# NOTES

## on

# REVELATION

## by

# JIM FLANIGAN

GW00643155

DECEM.
Published by
GOSPEL TRACT PUBLICATIONS
411 Hillington Road, Glasgow G52 4BL

Copyright © 1987
Assembly Testimony

ISBN 0 948417 21 8

Reprinted November 1991

Typeset, printed and bound by
GOSPEL TRACT PUBLICATIONS
411 Hillington Road, Glasgow G52 4BL

# CONTENTS

# FOREWORD

"The coming of the Lord draweth nigh" so says the Spirit of God through the pen of James, the Lord's brother, in the epistle which was in all likelihood the first New Testament document to be written. After that initial declaration the rest of the New Testament abounds with references to the Coming of the Lord and associated events. We are living in days of crises, the world rushes swiftly to its inevitable doom. Christendom continues with its compromise, departure and corruption, seeking a maximum of unity and a minimum of doctrine — indeed a unity without God. It is rapidly preparing for its part in the harlot system of a coming day. Among Christians the love of many waxes cold, and truths once held as the precious things of God are being sold for a "mess of pottage" in the market of worldly ease. These are indeed last days and perilous times. Above it all let us rejoice, God has said "Yet have I set my King upon my holy hill in Zion" (Psa. 2:6).

In days like this the lamp of Prophecy shines brightly in a dark place. In the increasing darkness men seek for light, for a ray of hope amid despair. The Book of the Revelation that promises a blessing even to those who read it, immediately focuses our minds on things future — Prophecy! Things to Come!

Just prior to and since the last war many unwise, rash statements have been made relative to world events and the truths revealed in the word of God. Preachers often with a minimum of Biblical knowledge and an amazing ingenuity and imagaination have brought prophetic study into disrepute. Prophetic truth was not given to make foolish men into prophets! Rather was it given in order that we might consider what manner of men we ought to be.

We must ever remember that the Holy Scriptures are the word of God, they must be read, meditated upon and carefully expounded in the fear of God, with the gracious help of the Holy Spirit. This book that I heartily commend to you, was written by my good friend Jim Flanigan and appeared over a period of time in the magazine "Assembly Testimony." It is not speculation, or wild imagination, but sober handling of the precious things of God. The readers of the magazine profited greatly from our brother's writings and many have expressed their conviction that the articles should be produced in permanent form for the help of the Saints. Our brother, who is an excellent expositor and a real Christian gentleman, has revised the series of articles which are now presented in book form. I heartily commend this book as a sane scriptural outline of the Book of the Revelation and am sure that it will be a real help to all its readers.

A.M.S.G.

# PREFACE

These "Notes" are the fruits of some forty years special interest in the Book of Revelation. I am indebted to so many brethren for help and encouragement during those years, but to three men in particular I am especially grateful.

When I was a very young Christian I was introduced to the Revelation by a Bible Class teacher in the Parkgate Avenue Gospel Hall, Belfast. It was my first acquaintance with this intriguing book. There was a strange mixture of fascination and fear. So much of what was being taught I could not understand. But it was an introduction, and I thank God.

Some ten years later, while living in Melbourne, Australia, I met a dear man who influenced me greatly. His knowledge of the text of Revelation was astounding. It could be safely said that there was not a verse in the book with which he was not familiar. Even those who would not agree with his interpretations admired his knowledge of the text. He used to say to me, "Read the Revelation; study the Revelation. It will affect your ministry; it will colour your Gospel preaching; it will mould your character. Whatever else you read, or don't read, read the Revelation." With his encouragement I continued, with deepened interest, to read and study.

Shortly after our return to Northern Ireland from Australia, there was an upsurge of Amillennialism in the Province. I turned for help to our late dear brother Mr David Craig. We spent hours together. He lent me, and eventually gave me, his large Chart on "The Book of the Revelation," and encouraged me greatly. So many of us revere his memory and thank God that we were privileged to know him.

7

If these "Notes" can help others, as others have helped me, I will be glad. I am grateful too, to my brethren of "Assembly Testimony" who have made them possible and available. We live in a dying dispensation, and a study of the Revelation and kindred scriptures is now more relevant than ever. May the Lord be pleased to bless, as He has promised to bless, the reading of this great Book. May we, as we study angels and demons and plagues and wars, not miss this, that this is the Revelation of Jesus Christ. May we find Him, and appreciate Him more and more.

Jim Flanigan
Belfast
6 July 1987

# Chapter 1

## AN INTRODUCTION

John, the Beloved, has been privileged to write for us three parts of our New Testament, and these are related to the Past, the Present, and the Future. From his memories of the past he has gathered precious clusters of fragrant things, and has given us the fourth Gospel. For our present guidance and help he has written for us three small letters. As the New Testament seer he has given us his Patmos visions in the "Book of the Revelation," sometimes called the "Apocalypse".

In his Gospel, John never once mentions his own name, but five times calls himself, "the disciple whom Jesus loved". In the Revelation, he five times refers to himself by name — "I John". It is highly unlikely that the writer of the Revelation could have so simply signed himself, with no additional, identifying, term or designation, had he not been the aged, sole-surviving Apostle who gave us the Gospel and the letters — the John so well known by first Century Christians. He is the Daniel of the New Testament, the man greatly beloved, of the Church Age.

Without doubt, the Apocalypse is the most neglected, most un-read book of the New Testament. Believers may often advance reasons why this is so, but there are many reasons why it ought not to be so.

*(i) This is the only book of prophecy in the New Testament.*

We have books which are Historical, and books which are Doctrinal; we have some which are Devotional, and some which are Practical; but only one book is purely

9

Prophetical. It is sad that the only book of prophecy in the New Testament should be so neglected.

*(ii) This is the final, closing, book of our Bible.*

There is undoubtedly a Divine arrangement in the order of the books of our Bible. Genesis was not the first to be written, but it is the obvious book to introduce all the others. Revelation was not the last to be written, but it is the great closing counterpart to Genesis. The comparisons and contrasts of Genesis and Revelation have often been pointed out. How much that has its beginning in Genesis, has its culmination in Revelation. How much finds its fruition in Revelation that had its roots and origin in Genesis. Like corresponding clasps on either side of a girdle, these two great books complement each other. They unite to form the complete circle of Divine revelation. Only the Apocalypse could intelligently be placed last as the capstone of Holy Scripture. We must not neglect this closing book.

*(iii) This is the only book which opens with a specific promise of blessing for those who read and obey.*

While this may primarily be a reference to public reading, in the days when not everyone had the ability or privilege to read personally; and while also the principle of blessing for obedience is everywhere in Scripture, nevertheless, this is the only book so to be introduced. We must not miss that blessing.

*(iv) This is the REVELATION of Jesus Christ.*

It is not "The Mystery", but "The Revelation". It is the Apocalypse, which means that it is an unveiling, an unfolding, of the Christ. Is it a revelation given *to* Him?

Or is it a revelation given concerning Him? Are both true? Either way, it is a revelation. Here is a rebuke to our neglect, and a great encouragement to read.

How often too, in this connection, is the title of the book misquoted. It is the "Revelation" — not the "Revelations". There is no "s". It is not a plural word. This is not quibbling, or unimportant. Many revelations indeed there may be throughout the book, revelations in every chapter, but these all blend together to become one harmonious Revelation of the Lord Jesus. It is one unveiling of Himself.

An analysis of this book is difficult. It does not readily lend itself to simple divisions and sub-divisions, as do some other books. So many crises, parentheses, climaxes, defy any straightforward analysis. There is however, one interesting way of dividing the visions.

Throughout the course of the Revelation, John's position and circumstances are changed several times. Indeed we find him in five different positions. The visions then given to him are accurately and absolutely in accord with his position at the time.

In chapter 1, John is bowed low at the feet of the Lord of the churches. On a rocky, barren island, so symbolic of our place of pilgrimage and testimony, he kneels at the Saviour's feet. Where better to receive the messages of chapters 2 and 3, concerning the ministry of the lampstands, the churches?

In chapter 4 his position is changed. He is caught up to the Throne. What more fitting place from which to see the workings of Sovereignty? From this glorious vantage point John will see the purposes of God being accomplished.

In chapter 13 his position is changed once again. He is now at the sea-shore. Here will he see the waves and billows of democracy rolling into anarchy and tyranny, and, rising out of the sea, the Dictator of the last days.

In chapter 17 there is a further change, and John is taken to the wilderness. In desert conditions he sees the great Babylon Mystery — a fitting prelude to his final position and the closing visions.

In chapter 21 he is taken to the mountain top. From this lofty viewpoint John sees the glory of the New Jerusalem and the ultimate bliss of the Christ and His people.

Five positions then, and five series of visions completely in harmony with the Apostle's circumstances. To summarise:

> Ch.1. At the Lord's Feet to learn the Principles of Testimony.
>
> Ch.4. At the Throne, to learn the Purposes of Sovereignty.
>
> Ch.13. At the Sea-shore, to see the Progress of Iniquity.
>
> Ch.17. In the Wilderness, to see the Power of Apostasy.
>
> Ch.21. On the Mountain, to receive the Promise of Glory.

The Book of Revelation is a book of symbols. The truths given us here are conveyed in the language of symbolism. So the opening verse states specifically. The word "signify", is literally "SIGN-ify" — to make known by signs. Our approach then, will be to see symbolism, unless, for some obvious reason, the passage should be taken literally. We shall find these symbols drawn from almost every part of life. There is symbolism from

(i) MATHEMATICS.

What a variety of numbers there is in Revelation! 2, 3, $3^1/_2$, 4, 5, 6, 7, 10, 12, 24, 42, 144, 666, 1,000, 1260, 1,600,

7,000, 12,000, 144,000, 100,000,000, and 200,000,000.
There is a predominance of the number "7".

(ii) ZOOLOGY.

Horses, Lambs, Lion, Calf, Leopard, Bear, Frogs,
Locusts, Scorpions, Eagle, Vulture, Fish, Serpent.

(iii) BOTANY.

Trees and Grass, Wheat and Barley and Grapes.

(iv) NATURE.

Mountains, Rivers, Seas, Fountains, Rain, Hail, Earthquake.

(v) ASTRONOMY.

Sun, Moon and Stars. Lightning and Thunder.

(vi) GEOGRAPHY.

Jerusalem, Babylon, Egypt, Sodom, the River Euphrates. .

(vii) MINERALS.

Gold (Lamps, Vials, Censer, Altar, Crowns, Cup)
Silver, Precious Stones, Pearls, Ivory, Wood, Brass, Iron,
Marble.

(viii) COLOURS.

Red, Green, Scarlet, Purple, Black, but especially
White.
There are, in this book of symbols, Men with Swords,

Reapers with Sickles, Trumpeters with Trumpets. There are Flutes, Lyres and Harps.

It is interesting, that in all the book of Revelation, there is not a single direct quotation from the Old Testament. Nevertheless, the book is saturated with Old Testament imagery, drawn especially from Isaiah, Ezekiel, Daniel, and Zechariah. For instance —

> The Glorified Christ of ch.1 is in Daniel ch.10.
> The Rainbow-circled Throne of ch.4 is in Ezekiel ch.1.
> The Scroll of ch.5 may be seen in Ezekiel ch.2 and Zechariah ch.5.
> The Measuring Reed, the Two Witnesses, the Two Olive Trees, and the Lampstands of ch.11 are in Zechariah ch.4.
> Beasts from the Sea, as in ch.13 are in Daniel ch.7.
> Gog and Magog are in Ezekiel chs. 38 and 39.
> The Great Assize of ch.20 is in Daniel ch.7.
> The New Jerusalem, the River of Life, and the Tree of Life, are in Ezekiel ch.47.

Many of these symbols are explicitly explained for us. For the rest, may we approach the book in a spirit of wondering humility, asking for Divine aid to know the mind of the Spirit.

May this great book become indeed to us — "The Revelation of Jesus Christ."

# Chapter 2

## EARLY VISIONS

Many of the truths of the Revelation are conveyed in an interesting "triplet" fashion. The divine number "3" is enshrined everywhere. This is especially so in chapter 1, where so much is structured around that number. We have, for instance —

*(i) The 3-fold Ministry of John. v.2.*

Is this a pattern for all true ministry at any time? Such is based upon the Word of God; it bears witness to the Lord Jesus; it is the measure of a man's personal experience.

*(ii) The 3-fold Beatitude. v.3.*

They that read, they that hear, they that obey, are blessed. It is, of course, the word for public reading to a congregation. In the days when literature and literacy were not so abundant as now, that was a blessed privilege indeed, to be the public Reader. It is still a privilege, and those who accept it are obliged to read distinctly, carefully, and reverently, remembering that true, proper reading, can be exposition in itself. The "hearing" and the "keeping" are linked together. It is assumed that those who hear will desire to obey — it is the way to blessing.

*(iii) The 3-fold Salutation. vv.4-5.*

From three Divine Persons the greeting of grace and

peace is conveyed. It is the heavenly "Shalom." From the
Father in all His Majesty, from the Son in all His Beauty
and Glory, and from the Spirit in all His Plenitude of
Power, the salutation comes.

*(iv) The 3-fold Appellation. v.4.*

"Him which is, which was, which is to come". Mr.
Newberry remarks that this is the nearest definition of
the great Name "Jehovah", combining the three periods
of existence in one divine Title. It is a paraphrase of the
unspeakable, unpronounceable Name, by which He
makes Himself known, Who has neither Past nor Future,
but lives as the "I am" in an eternal Present.

*(v) The 3-fold Presentation of the Lord Jesus. v.5*

The Son is the Faithful Witness of the past. He Who
witnessed a good confession before Pilate, (and the
world), is now the First-begotten of the dead in
resurrection glory, and in a day yet to come He will be
manifested and vindicated as Prince of the Rulers of the
Earth.

*(vi) The 3-fold Ministry of the Lord Jesus. vv.5-6.*

By Him, we have been loved, loosed, and lifted. Loved,
in spite of our sins. Loosed, by His Death, from our sins.
Lifted, out of our sins to a Royal Priesthood with all its
privileges. And of course, as is well known, the love of
Christ is a continuing thing — the word is "loveth" us.
His love is ever present.

*(vii) The 3-fold View of His Return. v.7.*

When He comes with clouds, whether clouds of saints

or vapour clouds, every eye shall see Him. What a vision for those alive at that moment. They also which pierced Him, not Jews only, nor Romans only, for Golgotha was the crime of the Gentile and the guilt of the Jew. All kindreds of the earth shall wail — the word is "tribes" of the earth. There will be a universal beating of the breast when He appears.

*(viii) The 3-fold Fellowship of Saints. v.9.*

There is a brotherhood, a companionship. What a comforting thought for the lonely John. A fellowship in present suffering, in future glory, and in patience while we wait. Through faith and patience we must enter the kingdom, and the companionship of kindred hearts helps us as we wait. May the Lord enable us to foster that mutual comfort and help so much needed by exiles in a hostile world.

*(ix) The 3-fold Majesty of the Son. v.18.*

He lives; He became dead; He is alive forevermore. Once He died — to live again. Now He lives — never to die. The Keys (a symbol of authority, Matt. 16:19; Rev. 3:7; 9:1; 20:1) hang at His Girdle.

> *"Worlds and worlds are hanging on His hands,*
> *Life and Death are waiting His commands —"*

He is superior to Death and Hades; He is the First and the Last.

*(x) The 3-fold Content of the Book. v.19.*

Things which John has seen; things which are; things which are to be after these things; such is the key for the opening of the Revelation. We shall use the key in a usual way, i.e. to open ch.1 first of all, then chs. 2 and 3, and then, after these things, ch.4 to the end. This will open to us an acceptable 3-fold division of the Prophecy.

Note also the three "Amens". There is an ascription of praise and glory to the Lord Jesus, v.6, and, — Amen! There is an announcement of His indisputable authority and power, v.18, and, — Amen! There is an anticipation of His return in glory, v.7, and, — Amen! So be it. The "Amen" becomes His very title, ch.3:14, since He is the fulfilment and confirmation of all God's purposes and promises.

Characteristically and fittingly, the first vision in the Apocalypse is a vision of the Lord Jesus. This also may be studied in a 3-fold way.

     (a) His Garments. His Girdle. His Sword.
     (b) His Hair. His Eyes. His Voice.
     (c) His Feet. His Hands. His Countenance.

— what a revelation of glory for an aged Apostle who remembered vividly the Garments stolen, the Head thorn-crowned, the Hands and Feet pierced and bleeding. How thrilling it must have been for John, who had witnessed the suffering, now to see the glory. Men may circumscribe John physically, in a Patmos only 10 miles by 6 miles, but he is now to be transported away from it all, and, in the Spirit on the Lord's Day, where better to begin than with a sight of the Lord Himself. In a state of spiritual ecstasy, liberated from the barrenness of Patmos, released from the visible world of the senses, John is lifted to the glory. What compensation for an aged saint being denied the usual privileges of the first day of the week.

The symbolism of the first vision is full of majesty and beauty, and we are again helped to an understanding of it by reference to other scriptures. The imagery of course, is Eastern, and Oriental. Perhaps our western minds need to be adjusted as we ponder. The Son of Man is in the midst of the "lampstands". Not the self-consuming "candlelight" as in our A.V. but the light of golden lamps whose light-bearing is nourished and maintained by oil. In a judicial character the Lord walks (ch. 2:1) in the midst. He is the Lord of the Lamps, the Master of Assemblies.

The long trailing robe is a token of dignity. It belonged to those in high office among men. Here is Manhood, in true dignity, in the Lord of the Churches.

The Girdle is of gold, and is around His breasts, not His loins. The girded loins were indicative of active service, and our Lord was no stranger to girded loins. But the girdle around the breast was the manner of the Sovereign, the Potentate, for whom others girded their loins and served. Let us see, in the girdled breasts, not the restraining of affection, as suggested by some, but rather, the evidence of Sovereignty whom others serve. John had once seen the same Lord Jesus robed in purple. He had seen Him too, girded with a towel. Then it was humility, but now the robe and the girdle are the symbols of dignity and sovereignty.

His head and His hairs are white, — like wool and like snow. Did John remember the Mount of Transfiguration? Did he recall the Ancient of Days whom Daniel saw (Dan. 7:9)? How often, with us, the white head tells only a story of age and decay; we must remember too, that it betokens wisdom, and experience, and knowledge. John had seen that Head bleeding, wreathed with thorns.

His eyes and His feet are both associated with Fire, and fire is ever associated with judgment. Eyes like a flame of fire, discerning, intelligently and infallibly, with feet like burnished brass — He will be active when judgment is necessary. Men may sometimes move in judgment when they have not the ability to properly discern. Men may sometimes discern correctly, and not have the moral strength to move in judgment. The Corinthians were guilty on both counts, judging when they had no right to judge, and failing to judge when judgment was needed.

But in the Lord the balance is perfect. His eyes discern infallibly. His feet move actively in necessary judgment.

His voice is majestic as the sound of many waters. As the myriad sounds and tones of the falling waters of a mighty cataract blend harmoniously together in one symphony — so the Voice of the Lord. All that He speaks, whatever the tone of His address, or the manner of His approach, all sounds out His glory and His authority. How clearly this is seen in the variety and diversity of the messages to the churches.

In His right hand He holds the seven stars. The stars are the angels. The double symbol indicates the responsible light-bearing element in the assembly. These He desires to hold authoritatively and protectively in His right hand. These He will deem accountable for the condition of the assembly, and through these the assembly will be addressed in every case.

From His mouth proceeded a sharp sword. The two-edged sword was a then familiar sight. It was the insignia of high office — the Roman Proconsul wore it. It is a familiar symbol to us, who, from Eph. 6:17; Heb. 4;12; Rev. 19:15, 21, know it to be the Word of God, penetrating, dividing, separating, searching, laying bare. It will be drawn especially against Pergamos, ch. 2:12, mixed with the world, her separation gone. Here are the two edges of impartiality, and the Lord jealous for the purity of the testimony and the affections of His people.

His whole countenance is as the sun at noon-day. It is glory indescribable and unbearable. It is the Mount of Transfiguration again. John had slept then; now he falls prostrate, as dead in the presence of the glory. But the divine touch enables him, as it had five times enabled Daniel, Dan. 8:18; 9:21; 10:10; 10:16; 10:18. He hears the first of a series of prohibitions — "Fear not", and he rises, by grace to give to us the messages to the seven selected assemblies. These letters follow in chapters 2 and 3.

# Chapter 3

## THE GOLDEN LAMPS

As is well known, chapters 2 and 3 of the Revelation are composed entirely of seven letters written to the seven assemblies named in ch. 1. The young believer should early learn the names of the cities, in order as the churches are addressed, and then learn to attach the meanings of the names, since these have a symbolic significance.

There are four interesting and profitable ways of approaching a study of these letters, viz. —

    1. HISTORICALLY    2. PROPHETICALLY
    3. PRACTICALLY     4. PERSONALLY

### 1. HISTORICALLY

These were letters written to seven actual, existing, literal assemblies functioning at that time. They were located in a geographic circuit in Asia Minor, which we now know as Turkey. Outside of the Revelation we have mention of only two of these assemblies, Ephesus, and Laodicea (Col. 4:15-16). The city of Thyatira is referred to in Acts 16, but not in relation to the assembly, which was not yet in existence at that time. Only of Ephesus have we any real knowledge apart from the Revelation. We have the record of the beginnings of the work there in Acts 19, and of course we have Paul's epistle to the assembly, written some ten years later. It is a sad reflection, that conditions so well known to us today, were actually prevalent in such early days of assembly testimony.

## 2. PROPHETICALLY

There appears to be what has often been called, a "Panorama" of the history of Christian profession. This we must consider in more detail as we peruse the letters, but here we offer five reasons to justify such a prophetic approach.

*(i) The significance of the number "7".* Why seven churches? Why seven only? There were others in this area. Why this particular seven? Is there not a prophetic significance in the divine selection of seven particular assemblies?

*(ii) These letters are an integral part of a book of prophecy.* The whole book is a prophecy, and the letters form part of that whole. It is not that the book begins in ch. 4 and a copy is sent to seven churches; the book begins in ch. 1 and the letters are contained in the body of prophecy. There must be a hidden prophetic meaning.

*(iii) The word "mystery" is attached to the letters.* This surely implies a deeper meaning.

*(iv) The analysis of ch. 1:19.* The "things which are" must be the things of chapters 2 and 3. In ch. 4:1 John is caught up to see the things which must be after "these things." The logical interpretation is that "these things" are conditions in the days of present testimony, as envisaged in the letters.

*(v) There is, in the letters, a most interesting series of allusions to Old Testament events.* These are noted in chronological order. From the Paradise, the Tree of Life, and the Fall, in Ephesus, reminding us of Eden; through the persecution and tribulation of Smyrna, suggestive of Israel in Egypt; to the reference to Balaam and to the Manna of the wilderness, in Pergamos. Then follows Jezebel, and

reference to Monarchy in Thyatira. In Sardis there is an echo of Zechariah ch.3, as we read of defilement, and white raiment, and in Philadelphia we have the City, the Temple, and a new Jerusalem, reminiscent of Nehemiah. But the age of testimony ends in blindness, in Laodicea, as did the days of the remnant. Those who came back from Babylon degenerated to the blind Phariseeism of our Lord's day. If the maxim is true, that history repeats itself, then here, in present day testimony, Old Testament history is being duplicated.

## 3. PRACTICALLY

Any condition, of any assembly, in any place, at any time, may be found here. If the problem is here, so too, is the remedy. In a practical way, each of us may see his assembly depicted here, somewhere in the letters, and find also, the answer to every distressing condition. Always that answer appears to be a fresh appreciation of the Lord and His Word. The problem in each case may indeed be different; the environment and circumstances may be varied; but always there is that same appeal to a renewed recognition of some aspect of His Person. This is the unvarying answer to our varying need.

## 4. PERSONALLY

"Every thoughtful believer will find himself mirrored here" — so it has been aptly remarked. So, I read the letters, interpret the condition to which each of them is directed, and ask myself the question — "Am I an 'Ephesian' believer, gone cold in heart?" or, "Am I a 'Pergamum' type, marked by a certain worldliness, my separation gone?" "Am I suffering, like Smyrna; or weak, like Philadelphia?" Whatever my state, there is an answer, and a remedy — Himself! In grace the Lord adapts His approach to suit the condition, but always the antidote for our failure is a renewed attachment to Him.

Apart from the specific messages and directions to each church, there are several great basic, fundamental lessons to be learnt here relative to assembly testimony.

(i) The Centrality, Supremacy, and Sovereignty of Christ. He walks in the midst. He is Lord. He alone has authority. He alone removes a lamp or threatens judgment. Twenty-four times in seven letters, our Lord says, "I will." He alone has this right.

(ii) The Responsibility, Autonomy, and Unity of the lamps. Their privilege is to shine for Him, and upon Him. They are individually responsible and accountable to Him, not to each other. But their joy, nevertheless, is to shine together, unitedly, in a common testimony to Him. Each in its own district, each on its own base, but together diffusing their light for His glory. There is no amalgamation. There is no federation. There is no union. But there ought to be the sweetest fellowship and harmony, and an interest and care for each other as together we bear witness to Him.

(iii) The continuity of assembly testimony. Right until the close of the period, the address is to the assembly. There may indeed be an appeal to the individual in the assembly, but still, the Spirit speaks to the churches (ch. 3:22). By all means let each individual believer see to his personal state and condition, but collective testimony has ever been the mind of God for His people, and we must foster and maintain 'House of God' character, so that He may dwell among us. A man's house is where a man resides, and rules, and rests. The assembly must be that for God. From the initial, apostolic, "Ephesian" days, through the centuries to the "Laodicean" end times, local assembly testimony continues. The word "church" or "ekklesia" is never used of the mass of believers on earth at any given time. It is used of the Church which is His Body, and it is used of the local company — a gathering of saints called out and called together to be His testimony,

His assembly, in a district. The term "church of God" is probably used exclusively in the New Testament of that local testimony. It is surely orderly for every believer to join himself to the assembly in his locality, and to feel his responsibility there; not passing other assemblies just to find a company more to his liking. How many problems might be solved; how many polarisations would be avoided, if each of us felt his responsibility to the assembly nearest to his home.

It is interesting to note the consistent symmetry in the structure of the seven letters. The basic pattern is the same in every letter.

(i) Each is prefaced by the command to John to write. Always the command is in the same form. If, in our Authorised version, there is a variation in the case of the Laodiceans, this is an A.V. rendering only, with little or no support in early manuscripts.

(ii) There is then a particular approach by the Lord, in a manner suited to the condition of the assembly. Under some part of the description given in ch. 1 the Lord addresses each church. In wisdom and in grace, He adapts to the needs of His people.

(iii) To each and every assembly He says, "I know," and based on His Divine (and therefore accurate) knowledge of the conditions, He conveys His message, sometimes commending, sometimes condemning, sometimes comforting, sometimes reproving.

(iv) There follows a promise to the overcomer. These promises again vary, but are consistent with the conditions and difficulties which the faithful have had to meet in testimony.

(v) Each letter concludes with an appeal which is worded so as to give a wider application to the message — "He that hath an ear, let him hear ..." That is, to all with spiritual perception the appeal is made. The Spirit is speaking to the churches. Initially, the letter may be addressed to one particular church, but the contents are, eventually, for all the churches, to be appreciated by every individual believer with a will to hear.

As is well known, the promise to the overcomer precedes the summons to hear, in the first three letters, but in the last four this order is reversed.

In two of the letters, Smyrna and Philadelphia, there is no reproof. This is not necessarily because there was nothing to reprove, but because the Lord, in grace, recognises the suffering of Smyrna, and the weakness of Philadelphia. In the circumstances, He will comfort and encourage, rather than condemn.

In the Laodicean letter, and perhaps, it may be argued, in the letter to Sardis also, there is no commendation. The sovereign Lord has His reasons for withholding praise from assemblies which ought to have known better, and whose condition was indefensible. In the other three epistles, to Ephesus, Pergamos and Thyatira, praise and reproof are mingled.

Before proceeding to the actual text of the letters, we append the suggested meanings of the names, with the hope that young believers will early learn to attach the meaning to each assembly.

- (i) EPHESUS ..... Desirable.
- (ii) SMYRNA ..... S-myrrh-NA. The sweet-bitterness of myrrh.
- (iii) PERGAMOS ..... Marriage. Mixture.
- (iv) THYATIRA ..... Continual Burning.
- (v) SARDIS ..... A Remnant escaping.
- (vi) PHILADELPHIA ..... Brotherly Love.
- (vii) LAODICEA ..... The Rights of the People.

There will be opportunity to enlarge upon, and involve, these suggested meanings in our study of the letters.

# Chapter 4

## THE LETTERS ... EPHESUS, SMYRNA AND PERGAMOS

Many interesting and profitable volumes have been written on the letters to the seven churches. What we offer here is but an introductory summary, and emphasis of the chief features of each epistle.

EPHESUS

Once known as the "Gateway to Asia," and the "Light of Asia," where Oriental religion and Greek culture converged, this great city was probably noted most of all for the magnificent Temple of Diana, one of the seven wonders of the world. The greater wonder of Ephesus, however, was that in such a place God had His "ecclesia," a company called out for Himself, from all the confusion and sin. It has been said of the work of the Lord in Ephesus, that Apollos prepared the soil, Paul planted it, Timothy cultivated it, John watered it, and God gave the increase; so, the church in Ephesus.

This letter comes from Him Who holds, sovereignly, the stars in His right hand. He walks, observingly, in the midst of the churches, nothing escaping His notice. He knew, and appreciated, their works, their labour, their patience, and their intolerance of evil men and evil things. He saw them busy and active and orthodox. In all this toil and endurance they had not fainted. This verb "fainted" is the root of the noun "toil," which is more correctly "weariness." There is a paradox, and a play upon words, as if the Lord would say, "Though weary, thou hast not wearied; toil for me has been no toil." They had toiled to the point of exhaustion but had not wearied. All this the Lord knew and appreciated, and commended, but there was something sadly lacking. Once, He might have said to this assembly, as was said to another, "... thy work of *faith*, and labour of *love*, and patience of *hope*," (1 Thess. 1) but sadly now, there was work, and labour, and patience, but a departure from a love that used to be. They had known a better love, but had left it, and if this was not evident to men, it was known to Him, who in an earlier letter to Ephesus had been presented to them as Bridegroom and Lover (Ephesians 5:25-32). Their bridal affections had waned now, and the Lord missed that. It was a serious omission, and not to be minimized, that the driving force of their activity should be duty and orthodoxy, and not love to Him. "I know," He says.

So serious is this heart departure, that it threatens the very existence of the lampstand. I stood one day to admire a magnificent rambling shrub, which covered the gable wall of a house in colourful glory. As I admired, the owner said sadly, "But look —," And he pointed to an injury by which, about four inches from the ground, the main stem had been severed. "What will happen?" I asked. The answer was sad and simple, "It will die," he said. We must return in love to Him. It is not enough to hate what He hates, though that is proper, but we must return to positive love to Christ. The gracious reward is, that Paradise, and Eden conditions, are restored. This is the third mention of Paradise in our New Testament (Luke 23; 2 Cor. 12).

Prophetically, here is a picture of those early days of Apostolic testimony, in which, so soon, there was departure in heart from Him Who desired so much the love and affection of His people.

## SMYRNA

The story of the suffering church is told in four verses. "Smyrna," is a derivation of "myrrh," which was an aromatic gum from Arabia. Myrrh was sweet to the smell, but bitter to the taste; a sweet bitterness; a bitter sweetness. It is mentioned in the New Testament, only in connection with the Birth, Death, and Burial of the Lord Jesus. From the bitter sufferings of the Lord's people there so often exudes a sweetness, that not only flows out to others, but rises to heaven too. So it was with Smyrna. Their suffering is twofold; present and future. They were enduring tribulation, poverty, and Jewish antagonism. They had yet to face imprisonment, trial, and death. One storm had not yet passed and another was about to break. In such circumstances the Lord, in grace, will not reprove or criticize, and the letter is all comfort and consolation. Omit too, the reference to "works," as in v. 9 (A.V.); this is usual in the other letters, but is not here. The Lord will go direct to their sorrows, and says, "I know thy tribulation." This is not the Roman "tribula," or lash, but a word meaning "to crush, or press," as grapes in a winepress, or as wheat in the mill stones. "I know," says the Lord. It is not the "I know" of omniscience, but the "I know" of experience. He Who had been to Gethsemane knew what crushing was.

> "Gethsemane, the Olive Press,
> And why so named, let angels guess!"

He knew their poverty too. He had been poor in Bethlehem and Nazareth. But how much better to be poor (but rich), than to be rich (but poor), like Laodicea (ch. 3:17). There are poor rich-men, and rich poor-men. The Laodiceans were poor rich-men. The Smyrnians were rich poor-men, like their Lord. For Him too, like them, there had been bitter persecution from the synagogue. The blasphemy of the Jews had now constituted them "the Synagogue of Satan." When, later, heathen opposition is spoken of, it is "the Throne of Satan." and when the trouble is heresy and apostasy, it is "the Depths of Satan" (ch. 2, verses 13 and 24).

What encouragement to them, that He Who experimentally knew their sorrows was alive! He was the First and the Last, greater than any Emperor of Rome (Isaiah 41:4; 44:6; 48:12). He too, had died — but lived! They must not fear the wrath of Caesars or Neros, with their presumptious claims to deity; Jesus was Jehovah, and knew their sorrows. Was there Jewish blasphemy? and heathen revilings? and Diabolical opposition? Well! Sixty years earlier other Jews had inspired Rome against *Him,* and Diabolos the Slanderer had been there too. They must take courage. For "ten days" they would be crushed. The suffering may be extensive, and intensive, but it was limited, and under His control. "He will not suffer you to be tempted above that ye are able." God is faithful; be *thou* faithful; and eventually, the reward is a victor's crown, whether of Rejoicing (1 Thess. 2) or of Righteousness (2 Tim. 4) or of Life (James 1) or of Glory (1 Peter 5) an incorruptible victor's crown (1 Cor. 9). and even if our faithfulness should result in physical death, we have the assurance that that is all — the second death can never touch us, we are His.

Perhaps, looking at the letter prophetically, there were indeed in those early days, ten distinct waves of persecution and martyrdom. Stake, sword, arena, and wild beasts, all played their part. Some of our brethren were burned as human torches, to light up the arena where others were compelled to fight with beasts. It is said that the final wave of persecution, the Diocletian, actually lasted ten years. But the blood of the martyrs was the seed of the church, and as we must now see, Satan changed his tactics and strategy.

## PERGAMOS

As Ephesus and Smyrna were centres of commerce, Pergamos (or Pergamum) was the capital of corruption. It was an illustrious city of wealth, fashion, and mystery, renowned for its learning, its refinement, its medicine and science. It boasted a library of some 200,000 volumes, second only in the world to the great library of Alexandria. It was the Cathedral City of Paganism, where Temples, Universities, and Palaces of Paganism abounded. There were temples to Juno, Jupiter, Venus, Bacchus, and Aesculapius. Here, first, in Asia, was set up the worship of the Emperor as God. The image of Caesar was venerated with the burning of incense. Here too, was the residence of the pagan Roman Viceroy. In a word, the throne of Satan was there in Pergamos.

In the midst of such corruption, the assembly had not denied either the Name or the Faith. They were true to the great doctrines relative to the Person of Christ and the gospel; and this, even when martyrdom had invaded their ranks. But what the Lord had against them was that they harboured and tolerated Nicolaitanism, which was Balaamism. The Lord distinguishes between the assembly and "them," but "they" were there, nevertheless. As Israel had had Balaam, this assembly had the Nicolaitanes. What had been "deeds" in Ephesus (2:6) was now accepted doctrine in Pergamos. Balaam was the devourer (such is the meaning of his name) who mixed the people of God with Moab. As a result of his evil counsel, 24,000 of Israel eventually fell under judgment. The Nicolaitanes were similarly devourers of the people. So the meaning of their name — conquerers of the laity. They were the false apostles of 2 Cor. 11, libertines, who led the people to impurity. This was a greater threat to the testimony than the persecution of Smyrna, and the Lord approaches them with the two-edged sword. His

people must be separate. He knows that they live where
Satan has his throne, and that testimony in such
circumstances must be difficult, but they must be
separate from it all, and He has against them that they
are tolerating those who would destroy that separation.
Idolatry and fornication, filthiness of the flesh and spirit,
are not compatible with testimony to Christ, "I will come
unto *thee*," He says, "and will fight against them."

To the overcomers, the promise is very sweet. They
shall eat the hidden manna. When? Perhaps now, but in a
fuller sense, then, when the battle and the pilgrimage are
over. The faithful shall share with God His appreciation
of His Son. How much has been hidden from us that we
would love to know. Thirty years of fragrant living in
Nazareth delighted the heart of God. Of those years we
know so little. Are they "hidden manna," which God will
share one day with His people? A white stone will be
given too. The interpretation is difficult. It may have
been a token of acquittal; or it may have been an honour
to one returning victorious from battle; it may have been
an award to a Freeman of the city; or a symbol of
friendship with names of friends inscribed upon it.
Whatever, we may be sure that here, in some way, is a
token of His pleasure and appreciation.

Prophetically, in Pergamos, we trace the dark days,
when "Church" and State were wedded together; when
being a Christian no longer meant variance with the
world, and the line of demarcation was obscured. May
the Lord help us to maintain a distinctive testimony until
He comes.

# Chapter 5

## THE LAST FOUR LETTERS

THYATIRA. Only in one other place in the New Testament do we read of Thyatira. In Acts 16 Paul arrives at Philippi and preaches by the riverside. Lydia is saved, and though she was then at Philippi, she is described as "a woman of Thyatira." Did she return there? Did she carry the news of salvation back there? We cannot tell, but eventually there is an assembly in her home town of Thyatir

The Lord approaches as "The Son of God," but He has at least ten other "Son" titles. He is Son of the Father, Son of the Blessed, Son of the Highest, Son of Mary, Son of Joseph, Son of the Carpenter, Son of David, Son of Abraham, Son of Man, Son of His Love. "Son of God" is full of Divine authority and personal glory. Whatever some brethren may think or say, the Jew certainly regarded it as a claim to Deity, (John 5:18). To them, it was not inferiority, but equality, and in such glory the Lord writes to Thyatira. He then displays the Divine attributes. There is Omniscience — Eyes like a flaming fire, discerning and discriminating. There is Omnipotence — Feet like burnished brass, trampling out what He hates.

Characteristically, the Lord will first of all commend whatever is commendable. He approves their works, their love, their ministry, their faith, their patience, and their works again (which were increasing). But they had a big problem. It could be summed up in one word — "Jezebel." How different was she to Lydia. Was she just a dominant woman in the assembly? or the wife of a prominent brother? (for the word "wife" may be implied)

or is the name symbolic? Either way, any way, Jezebel
was their problem. The original Jezebel is one of the most
wicked personalities in Bible history. She was an
idolatress; a persecutor; a murderess; a thief; a liar; a
hypocrite; an unscrupulous, unprincipled Sidonian Prin-
cess who married King Ahab, and introduced Babylonianism into Israel. In great subtlety she introduced the Baal
mysteries *alongside* the worship of Jehovah, and so the
seduction began. There was a Jezebel person or system in
Thyatira. The same persists until this day, seducing from
Christ, from Calvary, from the Word of God, from the
simplicity of His Truth. These she would replace with
other mediators, with ceremonies, rites, rituals, traditions,
phihlosophies, reasonings. It is the "deep things" of
Satan now. But there is a remnant. May the Lord help us
to insist like Paul, that in the midst of it all, we shall know
nothing but Christ crucified (1 Cor. 2:2).

The Lord appeals to the remnant — "Hold fast till I
come." There is a reference also to the morning star. Is
this the first mention of the Rapture in the letters? Their
encouragement is the prospect of sharing His glory
when the days of rejection are over. The men who were
true to David in Adullam, were closest to him when he
was vindicated. But note that from this point in the
letters, the appeal to him "that hath an ear" is the last
thing in each letter. It is an appeal now to a remnant.

SARDIS. Thirty-five miles from Thyatira, south-east,
lay the city of Sardis. Once a famous city, built on a
plateau, on a narrow ridge of mountain, its position
made it almost unassailable. It was an imposing sight;
walls and towers, temples and houses and palaces filling
the elevated plateau 1500 feet above the plain below. But
in 549 B.C. it was captured by Cyrus of Persia. One of
Cyrus' soldiers discovered a secret path of steps cut into
the cliff face. Silently, at night, the Persian troops
ascended one by one. There was no guard or sentinel at

the top, as this was deemed unnecessary, and when the citizens awoke next morning their proud citadel had been captured. "I will come on thee as a thief in the night." Prophetically, Sardis is a picture of dead Protestantism. We must distinguish between Protestantism and the Reformation — they are not synonymous terms. The latter was a divine movement, the former is a human system.

Sardis had forgotten. So has Protestantism. She has forgotten the Inspiration of Holy Scripture; she has forgotten the Deity of Christ; she has forgotten His Virgin Birth and His Sinless Humanity, and His miracles too. His Cross and His Resurrection, and the subsequent pardon for the guilty are all forgotten truths with her. Conveniently too, she has forgotten eternal punishment, the doom of the lost. Indeed, perhaps every fundamental truth is forgotten somewhere in the great system. The call is to remember, and to repent, or to be suddenly taken unawares by His coming, as was the Sardis of old by Cyrus. This is not the Rapture, but a judicial coming to them. They had a reputation, that they lived; in fact, great Protestantism is dead, and her works are incomplete.

The promise to the remnant, a few, is that they would walk in white with Him Whose garments were white and glistering on the Mount of Transfiguration; and if men were rejecting them, because of Him, and erasing their names from the registers of worldly society — never mind, there was another Book, in which their names were inscribed indelibly and eternally. Rejoice! Your names are written in Heaven, and one day the Father and His angels will acknowledge your faithfulness.

## PHILADELPHIA

The word means "Brotherly love." There are six other occurrences of the word in the New Testament (Rom.

12:10; 1 Thess. 4:9; Heb. 13:1; 1 Peter 1:22; 2 Peter 1:7 twice). God speaks through the meaning of the name. Philadelphia is an evangelical and ecclesiastical awakening of brethren from out of the deadness of Sardis. No doubt we have seen it in the thrilling history of the 19th Century. Note the number "3" again, as we have noticed it in chapter 1.

1. *The 3-fold Character of the Lord.*

(i) HOLY. Intrinsically so—Holy, Holy, Holy (Isaiah 6 and Rev. 4). Whether in awful Godhood, or incarnate in impeccable Manhood, He is thrice holy.

(ii) TRUE. He is, as we should be, girded always with Truth.

(iii) SOVEREIGN. He has authority to open and/or to shut. We rest in this. He is behind the scenes. He has the Key to all the treasures.

2. *The 3-fold Character of the Assembly.*
(i) WEAKNESS. They had little strength, but they entered the door which He had opened, like the early Jerusalem fishermen-preachers.
(ii) STEADFASTNESS. They had kept His Word —how much He appreciated that.
(iii) FIDELITY. They had not denied His Name. Among men, in the world, His Word is denied and His Person assailed. They had remained true to both.

3. *The 3-fold Comfort.*
(i) "I WILL KEEP." Twenty-four times in seven letters the Sovereign Lord says, "I will." His promise here is, to keep; and even when the trial is

universal, He will keep us too, from that very hour.
(ii) "I WILL MAKE." The Jew, the synagogue, will ultimately have to bow to this — that Christ loved the Church.
(iii) "I WILL COME." The Morning Star will appear. His personal coming will assure our deliverance from the hour of tribulation. Meantime, guard "thy crown." May this not be a crown of present testimony, rather than a future reward?

4. *The 3-fold Challenge.*

Overcome! — and I will make you a pillar (you who have little strength); in the Temple (you who have been persecuted by the synagogue of Satan). I will inscribe upon you —
(i) THE NAME OF MY GOD. As the sculptor engraves his name upon his work, so are we His workmanship. "Mine!" says the engraven name.
(ii) THE NAME OF THE CITY OF MY GOD. Twenty years earlier Jerusalem had been destroyed. The overcomer would have citizenship in an abiding City.
(iii) MY OWN NEW NAME. His Name shall be in their foreheads (Rev. 22). Will there be continuing fresh revelations of His glory? Eternally, new disclosures of His Beauty?
Let us be Phildelphian, true to Him in the midst of failure and darkness.

LAODICEA. The very sound of the Name is ominous. Laodicea has become a synonym for the lukewarm satisfaction of the last days. Of the seven assemblies, only Laodicea and Ephesus are mentioned elsewhere in scripture. Was the letter *from* Laodicea, referred to in Col. 4:15, actually the epistle to the Ephesians? an encyclical letter which had gone first to Ephesus, then to Laodicea, and then to Colosse? Would not these two epistles, to Ephesus and Colosse, in fact save us from Laodicean conditions? It is an interesting question, and searching too.

Notice once again, how predominant is the number "3" in this letter also. The presentation of the Lord is three-fold. There are three aspects of the self-sufficiency of the church. There are three charges concerning its condition (which she did not know). There are three courses of action which the Lord counsels.

Our Lord is introduced as "The Amen." How fitting is this in the closing letter. Here is finality and completeness. In Isaiah 65, Jehovah is referred to as "The God of the Amen." As we may say "Amen" to express our full agreement and approval of another man's statement, so Christ is the Amen to all the truth of God. He is not only the final word, but He ratifies and endorses every promise and precept and stated purpose of God. He is the faithful and true Witness. How does this contrast with the failure and pretensions of the Laodiceans? He is the Beginning, the Originator, the Author, of the creation of God — the Fountain-Head. He is the Uncreated, Who created all. He is the Eternal, from whom all else springs.

There is nothing to commend in Laodicea. They were rich, in a material sense, but as we have seen, they were poor rich-men in contrast to the rich poor-men of Smyrna. What makes their condition very sad is that they did not know. They were "poor" — the word is that for destitution, — and they did not know. They were blind, and like the Pharisees, they did not know. They were naked, wretched in their rags, but insisting "I am rich ... and have need of nothing." "I know," says the Lord, and He appeals. "Buy of Me" He says. But are His blessings not free? Let us remember that making room for Him will always cost something. He offers riches, vision, and dress. Riches that will abide; vision to see ourselves, and Him. Dress — fine, white, and pure. How tender and gentle is His appeal. How reminiscent of that in the Song of Songs 5:2 —"Open to Me, My love." How many of us listened for years to the appeal of Rev. 3:20 before we knew that it was not a call to the unconverted, but an appeal to an assembly. He, of Whom it is recorded, that "He came unto His own, and His own received Him not;" He, to whose earthly parents at Bethlehem someone said "No room," is now, at the end of the dispensation, outside, knocking. May we make room for Him now. If we do, He will make room for us, and we shall share His throne.

In the next chapter, that Throne is dramatically brought to our view.

# Chapter 6

## THE THRONE

The Throne of God is mentioned twelve times in chapter 4, and everything else in the chapter is related to that Throne. Nothing is seen apart from the Throne; everything is dependent upon the Throne. As we have seen in an earlier study, John's position is changed here, he is removed, at least in spirit, from the rocky barrenness of Patmos, and in the glory he will now learn, that, in spite of the power of Rome and the Caesars, there is a greater Sovereignty. God, in supreme authority, is still on His Throne, ordering everything for His own glory. This, in fact, is the meaning of sovereignty — a God Who does what He wills, when He wills, where He wills, how He wills, for whatever reason He wills; a God Who is answerable to no one, accountable to none. What a comfort to know, that such sovereignty is interested, not only in Nations and Empires, but in the daily lives and affairs of His people. May we be helped to rest in that sovereignty in all our perplexities and sorrows.

To emphasise the relation of everything to the Throne, five prepositions, or prepositional clauses, are used —

(i) *Upon the Throne* — Deity sitting in inscrutable splendour.
(ii) *Round about the Throne* — a Rainbow, and twenty-four crowned elders, and four strange living creatures.
(iii) *Out of the Throne* — lightnings, and thunderings, and voices.

(iv) *Before the Throne* — seven lamps of fire, a sea of glass, and the proffered crowns of the elders.

(v) *In the midst of the Throne* — the four living ones, who also surround the Throne; and, as we shall see in ch. 5, a little Lamb.

The whole chapter, therefore, with its peoples and events, is associated essentially with God's Throne.

The Throne is *set*. Men may challenge sovereignty, but men ought to know that sovereignty is really unchallengeable. "They shall perish; Thou remainest." The Throne is set in Heaven while earth rolls on in her confusion. The Throne-sitter is, in essence, indescribable, but John sees glory like the glory of the Jasper and the Sardine stones. In the reverse order, these stones were the first and last on the breastplate of Israel's High Priest, (Ex. 28). The ruby-red Sardius was first, the brilliant Jasper, with its purplish hue, was twelfth and last. It has often been pointed out, that if the names engraven on the stones of the Breastplate were ordered according to birth (as on the onyx stones on the Priest's shoulders) then the Sardius had the name of Reuben upon it, and the Jasper had the name of Benjamin. In both of these names the little syllable "Ben" occurs, which means "Son." This is interesting. When Jacob's first-born arrived (Gen. 29) they said, "Behold, a son," and so, his name, "Reuben." Perhaps, as we look to the Throne-sitter, we too shall say, "Behold, a Son." Is this the only way, in fact, in which we shall ever see God — by contemplating the Son? When Jacob's youngest was born (Gen. 35) the mother, Rachel, died, but before her death she named the baby "Ben-oni," which means, "Son of my sorrow." After her death, (and she died at Bethlehem) the father looked at the infant and said, "Not Ben-oni, but Benjamin" — "the Son of my right hand." This is the first mention of Bethlehem in our Bible; a child is born and a mother dies. From Bethlehem there came another Son. His mother, Israel, only ever knew Him as a Man of Sorrows, but to the Man of Sorrows the Father has said, "Sit Thou on my right hand." Ben-oni has become Benjamin. The Son is upon the Throne.

The emerald rainbow haloes the Throne. Surely here is the symbol of mercy, and pity, and the faithfulness of the Covenant-keeping God. The rainbow is "round-about" the Throne, complete. We never see the rainbow complete because, with our feet on earth, our vision is interrupted, and we cannot view the completeness. But the purposes of God are complete and eternal nevertheless, and one day we shall know it to be so, when, like John, we are caught up to the same glory. There too, we shall be better able to appreciate, for this rainbow is not a dazzling spectrum of colour, but rather of that green which is so easy to look upon and so soothing to the eye. We shall, in heaven, delight to dwell on those glories of the Divine character which down here we cannot rightly comprehend.

Around the Throne John saw an array of twenty-four other thrones, (it is the same word), and seated upon these were the twenty-four elders whose identity has ever been a matter of dispute. They are, of course, mentioned many times in the Revelation from ch. 4 through to ch. 19. What we do know of them is this —they are, as early as ch. 4, seated, robed, and crowned; in a word, rewarded. They are distinct from the angels (ch. 5:11). They are distinct from the saints of the great tribulation (ch. 7:13). They intelligently appreciate the purposes of God. They cannot be Old Testament saints, since these are not raised or rewarded, until the King comes (ch. 11:15-18; Dan. 12:12-13). Is it not interesting, that all the references to these elders are found in that section of Revelation in which the Church is viewed as being in Heaven, i.e. chs. 4-19? Do they not symbolise that Kingdom of priests, who, having completed their course of testimony in chs. 2 and 3, have now been translated to the immediate Presence, and are even closer than the angels?

The Throne is alive with lightnings, thunderings, and voices. The God of Sinai still lives! But before His awful Throne, and in intimate association with it, the seven Lamps of Fire burn. Here, no doubt, is the seven-fold fulness or plenitude of the Holy Spirit, in a ministry of holy liaison between God and men.

The Sea of Glass is there. The crystal purity of the Holiness of God is spread before His throne. No speck of defilement may remain unnoticed here. No spot or stain or suggestion of sin may pass undetected in the approach to the Throne. The crystal sea reflects the light from the Throne and from the lamps of fire, and here sin cannot be. How beautiful, that on that same Sea of Holiness, in a later chapter, the saints actually stand and sing! The righteousness which once debarred us from the awful Presence, now gives us a standing before God.

The four "living ones" are now contemplated. The word "beast" in our A.V. could be misleading. It is not the same word as in ch. 13. There we must leave the word unchanged, to convey to us all the beastly characteristics of the men there envisaged, but here in ch. 4 it is different, and is simply "living creatures." Who are they? What are they? Are they Cherubim? Are they Seraphim? Is there a difference? They are certainly intimate with the Throne, with a very full knowledge of the purposes of God — eyes before, behind, and within. They bear the likeness too, of that Son Who now sits upon the Throne, with their lion-like majesty, their ox-like patience in service, the intelligence of true manhood, and the rapidity of the eagle soaring in flight. As we shall see in ch. 5, the ministry of these holy beings is akin to the ministry of the cherubim, heavenly guardians of God's righteousness, and the holiness of His Throne and character. Ceaselessly, restlessly, they proclaim that holiness. It is the holiness of the Great Triunity — Holy, Holy, Holy. It is the Majesty of the Lord God Omnipotent, in whose terrible Name is embraced the past, the present, and the future. He lives "for ever and ever" to the ages of the ages. How many times does this expression occur in the Revelation. It is the strongest way possible in Greek to express eternity, perpetuity. The living ones acknowledge this and accordingly ascribe glory, and honour, and thanksgiving. The elders associate with that praise and spontaneously offer their crowns of victory to the Throne-sitter. He is worthy. He it was Who gave to them the privilege of representing Him on earth, and gave them golden crowns for so doing. Now, in heaven, they return to Him what He originally gave. Every created thing comes from Him, and the glory must go back to Him. How like the great doxology of Rom. 11:36 — "of Him, and through Him, and to Him, are all things." He is the source of all, and the channel, and the stream, and the great Originator to which everything must eventually return for His pleasure. To Him be the glory, for ever. Amen. This is true worship. May we seek to learn more, down here, of that which shall be, up there, our occupation forever. May our lives be governed, our service be rendered, our burdens be borne, and our characters moulded, by this wonder of wonders, that soon we shall, by sovereign grace, be in the Presence of the Throned One, and in His Presence be at home.

# Chapter 7

## THE LAMB AND THE BOOK

It is important to note the continuity of chapters 4 and 5. The chapter division should be ignored. Chapter 4 is but a prelude; it is the ante-chamber, the vestibule, to the glory of chapter 5. It is important too, to remember that the events of these chapters are yet future. While we may delight to see the present glory of the Lamb depicted here, nevertheless, the events are strictly future, and await the calling home of the Church.

In the opening verse of chapter 5, a minor, but important, change must be made in the text of our authorised version. The scroll is "ON" the Hand of the Throne-Sitter, not "IN." To see the scroll as being held "IN" His Hand, is to miss the beauty of the scene. The scroll is lying "ON" His Hand, extended, offered, to any who has the right and ability to take it. What is this scroll, with all the appearances of a sealed legal document? Surely it must be more than just a book of prophecy (as suggested by some). John would hardly have sobbed as he did just because there were events yet unrevealed. Have we not here rather, the Title-Deeds to a mortgaged earth? — the Rights to a world which has been ruined by sin? For centuries this old earth has been in a state of neglect and disrepair because of Adam's sin. Man has forfeited all title to it. But God's purpose from the beginning has been that it should be under the rule of Man, and here He is still extending, offering, the Title-Deeds to a worthy one. But there are conditions written in here. There must be ability and power to put the property in order. "Who can do it?" cries the Angel. "Who is worthy?" "Who is able?" The call resounds through earth and heaven with no response. The centuries have witnessed the puny attempts of Caesars and Neros, and many a Dictator, at world rule. The world has yet to see the greatest usurper of all. But John weeps, and angels wait, and principalities and powers watch, and none is found worthy. From the Universe of Science, Politics, Philosophy, Arts and Religions none is forthcoming. The sublimest power is necessary, and none has it; and still, the Title-Deeds lie offered on the hand of the Throne-Sitter.

One of the elders speaks to the weeping Apostle. "Weep not," is the exhortation. What a story of tears and sorrow this world has seen. Since the first recorded tears of Genesis 21:16 not only mothers like Hagar, but fathers too, and prophets and Kings, and apostles, have joined in the weeping. It has been a long, sad era of tears, but now, One has been found to dry the tears of the centuries — a Worthy One! The Lion of the Tribe of Judah! (Gen. 49). The Root of David; David's Son and David's Lord. Not only "offspring of David" but "Root of David" too (Rev. 22). He sprang from David, but He was before David. John looks through his tears, as Mary did long ago in the garden, and sees, not the Lion of Judah, but the Lamb of God, in the midst of the Throne. As is often pointed out, it is a diminutive word here — a little Lamb. The marks of sacrifice are upon Him, as if freshly slain. The memory of Calvary will ever be fresh in Heaven. But there is power too. The seven horns of Omnipotence, and the seven eyes of Omniscience are seen. Here, combined in the little Lamb in plenitude, is Right and Power, Authority and Ability, and there now follows what has been called "the sublimest individual act in the book of Revelation" — "He came, and took the book, out of the right Hand of Him that sat on the Throne."

It is the signal for the great outburst of praise. The

heavens reverberate: Elders and Angels join in "the song with which the heavens ring," and all exalt the Lamb. He is the theme and substance, and subject and object of the worshipping host, and at least one hundred and four million voices proclaim His worth. (Ten thousand times ten thousand, and thousands of thousands.) Harps and incense bowls are the fitting symbols of the praise and adoration of the saints and they sing the song of redemption.

If the A.V. text of verses 9 and 10 is correct, then, conclusively, the elders were not angels, but redeemed men. Some, of course, will not accept the accuracy of this text, and will see the song as a general ascription of praise to One who has redeemed men by His Blood. The redeemed ones are Royal Priests, destined to reign.

A myriad voices join in a seven-fold ascription of praise. What a reversal of the earthly story is this exaltation of the Lamb. Power and strength to Him Who was slain in apparent weakness; riches and wisdom to Him who lived and died in poverty and ridicule; honour and glory to Him Who bore the shame; blessing to Him Whom men blasphemed. And the Universe joins in the song, and repeats the substance of the great doxology, and the sound re-echoes again and again as the Lamb is extolled.

The living creatures are here too. If we equate them with the Cherubim, then what a scene is this. For centuries, since they first stood at the gate of Eden (Gen. 3) the Cherubim have blocked the way back to God. They have stood in Tabernacle and Temple, watching, guarding. They have defied man to draw near, except on God's terms. They have stood in the way to the holiest. But now they watch in wonder. A Man has gone up to the Throne — the Man of Calvary. He has approached the Throne in His own right and has taken the scroll. The living ones have but one word to say — "AMEN." They acquiesce. These holy guardians of God's rights have no complaint. The Lamb has a right to the Title-Deeds, and they bow in agreement as He takes them.

The elders worship again, and in the next chapter the scene will shift again from Heaven to Earth, so that we may see the unfolding of events as the Kinsman-Redeemer deals with the property and makes preparation for the Millennial Age.

# Chapter 8

## THE BEGINNING OF SORROWS

In Chapters 4 and 5 of the Revelation, John has been in Heaven, contemplating events which are preparatory to the Great Tribulation. The Church has been raptured; the Lamb has taken the Book; all Heaven has reverberated with praise. Now, from the glory, in ch. 6 John will see the beginning of sorrows on earth, as the seals are broken and the story of the days of vengeance is unfolded. It is noteworthy, that throughout all this great middle section of the Revelation, there is no mention of Church or Churches. How prominent they were in chapters 2 and 3, but the days of their testimony are over. They are now "conspicuous by their absence" —the saints of this mystery period are not on earth any more. We are now to be occupied with the "things which shall be after these things." The Church is in the glory. It is essential that, somewhere, in the Revelation, we must see the Rapture of the Church. The only feasible place is at the beginning of chapter 4 — "Come up hither!"

The Lamb now breaks the first seal, and the Living One thunders the summons, "Come." (see R.V.). In response, a white horse appears, his rider armed with a bow. A victor's crown is given him, and he rides on from strength to strength, conquering and to conquer. Some have interpreted the first rider as Christ Himself, but such an interpretation is not consistent with the scenes of judgment, bloodshed, and famine which follow in the train of the white horse. Rather should we see here, the advent of the Prince that shall come (Daniel 9:26), whose victory is, initially, a bloodless victory. With fair words and flatteries, with deceits and vain promises, he gains his power, until, as supreme despot of a resuscitated Roman Empire, he wields a control which is world wide. If his Kingdom has geographical boundaries, his influence has not, and as we shall see later in our studies, he is virtually a world Ruler.

So, with white horse and bow (but no arrows!) there is no suggestion of slaughter. Here is the arrival of the superman, whose assurances of peace and prosperity appeal to a weary world. Is not this man, and his anti-Christian system, that for which the world has been waiting and searching. He appears to be the answer to earth's problems, and, in at least a large section of that troubled earth he is assured of a ready acceptance. But the peace is not to last.

At the breaking of the second seal, and in response to the second "Come," a red horse comes forth. In the purposes of Sovereignty his mission is to take peace from the earth. This strengthens the suggestion that the first horseman has inaugurated peace of a kind. A sword is given to the rider of the red horse — a great sword. In keeping with the symbolic colour of his steed, he is responsible for bloodshed and slaughter. It is warfare too, of the most dreadful kind — civil warfare. It is not just nation against nation, or kingdom against kingdom. It is "that they should slay one another." The peace has been short-lived, and now there is unleashed a time of lawlessness and murder. Those days are unparallelled for cruelty and savagery.

The third horse is black. It is the colour of mourning, of famine, and of death (Lamentations 4:4-8; 5:10; Jeremiah 14:1-2). Famine is almost a logical sequence to war. If men are fighting, they are not sowing, planting, or reaping, and the inevitable dearth follows. The rider carries a pair of balances, and a voice from the midst of the Living Ones tells of the scarcity of the daily necessities of life. "A measure of wheat for a denarius."

The denarius, or Roman penny, was the common daily wage. A measure of wheat was apparently what a labouring man could have eaten at one meal. If, instead of wheat, he chose to buy the cheaper grain, barley, he may have three meals of this. A day's wages for a loaf of bread! And nothing left for the purchase of other requirements for home and family. What distress, confusion and trouble.

To increase the sorrow, the oil and wine are unaffected; the luxuries of the wealthy are untouched. So will be aggravated the ever present tension between the classes. What jealousies and envies will be fostered by this apparent inequity, that the necessities of the masses are in scarce supply while the luxuries of the rich are in abundance. Nothing could be more calculated to add to the civil unrest of those troublous times.

When the fourth horse comes forth he is described as "a pale horse." It is probably the ghastly, unearthly, pale green, which has been likened to "the colour of putrefying flesh." We are not left to ourselves to search for an interpretation —"His Name was Death." He is closely followed by Hades, called by some, "His Hearse," and by others, "His Stirrup Rider." Eventually, Death and Hades will be cast into the Lake of Fire (ch. 20:14), but meantime, they ride on, the logical, inevitable, aftermath to war and famine. It is easy to picture the triumph of Death and Hades, in days when scant diet and the lack of nourishing food will make men vulnerable to disease, and perhaps increase too, the ravages of wild beasts hungrily looking for food.

As the fifth seal is broken, we look again to heaven, but what we see and hear in heaven is but a fresh reminder of what is happening on earth. We see the martyred dead of the tribulation period; we hear them cry for vengeance. They are at the foot of the altar, where the blood of the sacrifices was wont to be poured out (Ex. 29:12; Lev. 4:7).

The blood of the martyrs cries out, like the blood of Abel,
that God should intervene. Surely their language
indicates that these are not believers of the present age,
and surely this is again, additional proof that the saints of
the mystery period are not at this time on earth. Listen to
the cry for vengeance. They call for God to avenge them.
They ask for divine judgment on their persecutors. And
note that they address God, not as Father, but as
Sovereign Lord, or Master. This is not the language of
the Church. It is language reminiscent of the imprecatory
Psalms and the cry of the Prophets. God *will* avenge. He
*will* act. There *will* be retribution. But not yet. They must
rest a little while, until the martyr roll is complete and
the mystery of God be finished.

The sixth seal is now broken, and the ensuing
catastrophic events are almost unthinkable. Whether we
take the phenomena to be typical or actual, symbolic or
literal, it is of little account; the scenes are fearful. Sun,
moon, and stars, mountains, hills, and islands, are all
affected. Royalty, nobility, aristocracy, afford no immun-
ity. Neither greatness nor authority, of office or person
will bring escape, and slaves and freemen are in this
together.

It is interesting, at this point, to compare the breaking
of the seals with our Lord's predictions in Matthew 24.
On the Mount of Olives our Lord outlined the sorrows
of these days. He spoke of deceivers, wars, famines,
death, martyrdoms, and earthquakes. There appears to
be a striking parallel between Matthew 24 and Revelation
6. Whether the language be figurative or not, earth-life
will be shaken at that time. Sun, moon, and stars, have
from the beginning been emblems of rule (Gen. 1:16;
Gen. 37:9). In the days of the sixth seal supreme
authority will topple. Subordinate or minor authorities
will consequently fall too, like unripe figs from the tree.
Apostasy and anarchy will triumph. The cosmos will

become chaos. It is the ultimate dreadful condition of a society that has rejected God. Men's hearts will fail them for fear. In vain will they search for a hiding place, for having rejected the will of God, there is nowhere to hide. In arrogant self-sufficiency men have waxen worse and worse. In the blasphemy of Beast-worship they sink deeper and deeper. Now, they would seek a refuge, but there is none. "Who is able to stand."

May the Lord make us increasingly grateful for that wondrous, sovereign grace, that has called us out from such society, so that now we wait, not for the World Ruler, but for Jesus, our Deliverer from the coming wrath. May He help us to be faithful while we wait.

For the breaking of the seventh seal, we must wait until ch.8. We must also decide whether the judgments under seals, trumpets, and vials, are consecutive or concurrent. We shall offer the view that the seals in fact cover the whole period up until the time of our Lord's appearing in ch. 19, and that the trumpets and vials have to do, in more detail, with the same period. In this case, seals, trumpets, and vials, are concurrent, not consecutive.

In the next chapter we come to the first of several great parentheses, and the purpose of this one is to let us see the triumphs of the cross, even during the dark days of tribulation. From out of that corruption and evil of the society of those days, great numbers will be saved. God will have glory even in the days of supreme opposition to His Person and Truth.

# Chapter 9

## THE TRIBULATION SAINTS

The Rapture of the Church is not expounded or developed in the Revelation; nevertheless, somewhere in the course of the book we must position this great event, and there are many sound reasons for placing it at the beginning of chapter 4. It may be helpful, at this point in our studies, to elaborate upon this, and to give reasons for believing that the Church must indeed be taken home before the storm breaks and the great tribulation begins. "Come up hither," is the call in ch.4:1, when the days of testimony are over at the end of ch.3. There are at least seven good reasons for seeing the translation of the Church at this point in the Revelation.

(i) *The Church is Unique.* The Church is a mystery creation of God in a mystery period unknown to the Old Testament prophets. It has an unique beginning at Pentecost; it has an unique story of testimony distinct from Israel; and there is no doubt that the word "mystery" attached to the Rapture in 1 Cor. 15:51 indicates an unique ending to the earthly story. To keep the mystery Church on earth during the long-predicted days of the seventieth week of Daniel ch. 9, is to confuse and confound things which must be distinguished. The unique mystery creation must be removed before God's stated programme of prophecy can be resumed.

(ii) *The Differences in our Lord's two parting Discourses.* Towards the close of His life and ministry, our Lord gave two great discourses. One we refer to as the Olivet Discourse (Matt. 24-25). The other is His Upper Room

Ministry (John 14-16). In both of these there is an emphasis on our Lord's return, but he would be a most naive reader who would not sense that the atmosphere, the content, and the tone and language of the two messages are very different. The answer, to some of us, seems very simple and reasonable. On the Mount of Olives, in public, our Lord is addressing His disciples as the remnant of the Nation, which undoubtedly they were. In the Upper Room, in private, our Lord is addressing the same men as the nucleus of the new Church, which again they undoubtedly were. On Olivet therefore, His ministry looks on to His return in glory. It has to do with Israel. In the Upper Room His ministry anticipates a prior personal coming for His own, to take them to Himself. It would be interesting to pursue a parallel of contrasts between these two ministries, but sufficient now to note that there is indeed a significant array of differences.

(iii) *The Tribulation is "Jacob's Trouble."* So it is called in Jeremiah 30:7. By no stretch of the imagination can the mystery Church be linked with Jacob's Trouble! Note that it is not even "Israel's" trouble, but "Jacob's." The old name of the unbelieving man and nation is purposely used. God is dealing with an unbelieving earthly nation after the translation of the saints of the mystery period.

(iv) *The Church is not on earth in Revelation after ch. 3.* We have before mentioned that in chs. 1-3 we read constantly of "the Churches;" "the Churches;" "the Churches." Is it not therefore remarkable, that when chapter 3 is ended there is now no more mention of Church or Churches until we see the Bride come out with the King in chapter 19, when the tribulation is over? Is it not equally remarkable, that if, as some believe, the Churches will still be here on earth during the tribulation, there is no instruction, no direction, no word of comfort, no exhortation, in fact, not even a mention! In all that great middle section of the Revelation which deals with the days of vengeance, the Church is absent. She is at home with the Lord.

(v) *The saved of the Tribulation Period are seen with* Jewish and Gentile distinctions. This brings us to chapter 7, at which, shortly we shall look in more detail: but sufficient to say now, that today, in the days of the mystery, the Body of Christ, there are no national distinctions in that Body. The old middle wall of partition has been removed; there is neither Greek nor Jew, circumcision nor uncircumcision, Barbarian, Scythian, bond nor free (Eph. 2:14; Col. 3:11). But in the days of Revelation 7 the old distinctions are seen again. This we must consider later, but the fact is important, and the reason is, that the Church, the Body, has gone.

(vi) *The Church is now the Temple.* Yet during the tribulation there will be a material, literal Temple, which Paul calls, "the Temple of God" in 2 Thess. 2:4. Is it not incongruous that God should have two temples on earth at the same time? Such would indeed be the case if the Church were here during the days of the great tribulation. The answer to the incongruity is to see the Church raptured away first, to make room, and place, and reason for, a material Temple as in days of old. Today, a Moslem Mosque stands on the Temple Mount in Jerusalem, but one day, some day, Israel will have her Temple again.

(vii) *The Difference in the Promises ending the two Testaments.* At the end of the Old Testament the promise to Israel is that Christ will come — like the Rising of the Sun (Mal. 4:2). At the end of the New Testament the promise to the

Church is that Christ will come — like the Morning Star (Rev. 22:16). Surely the accuracy of the symbolism is beautiful. As the night of Church testimony draws to a close, we look for the Morning Star. As the Day of millennial splendour approaches Israel will watch for the rising of the Sun. Between the appearing of the Morning Star and the rising of the Sun lie the dark dreary hours of tribulation.

We conclude, that although the Rapture of the Church is not the burden of the Revelation, nevertheless we must place it somewhere in the book, and the most obvious and satisfactory place is at the beginning of chapter 4.

But all this now raises the question — "Who then, are the saved of chapter 7?" Two companies are introduced in this chapter. There is a numbered company saved from out of Israel, and there is an innumerable company saved from out of the Gentile nations. Who are they? To what message have they responded? Who preaches the message? These are interesting and necessary questions which must be asked and answered.

First we must be assured that these are souls who have not heard the gospel during this age. Those who hear the gospel in this age of grace and wilfully reject it are damned. There is no second chance for such after the Rapture. 2 Thess. 2:10-12 makes it abundantly clear that to refuse the truth is to prefer the lie, and God will send strong delusion for those who have refused His offer of grace in the gospel. To reject Christ now, is to bow to the Beast when the Church has gone. There is no alternative. These saved ones of Revelation 7 are not those who have been left behind for some change of mind or late repentance.

But there is no problem. It is reckoned that at any given time there are about two-thirds of the world's population who have never heard the gospel. That is a staggering figure of some thousands of millions. This must include many sincere Jews, and it is easy to anticipate that with the trauma of the Rapture, and the consequent world-wide upheaval, and the search for explanation as to what has happened, that many earnest Jewish seekers will turn to the New Testament writings, to discover, in fact, that Messiah has already come, and has been rejected, and has built His mystery Church, and has taken it home. Many such Jews will receive Him, and will become, like Simeon and Anna, the testifying remnant to speak of Him, and to spread among Israel and the Nations the truth of His gospel.

Until such are sealed for God, no hurt can come. Four angels hold back the winds, and the servants of God are sealed. Millions of others will eventually be branded with the Beast's mark, but God has His servants, sealed in their foreheads.

It is important to note, that the basis of salvation is the same in every age — "the Blood of the Lamb." Salvation is ascribed to the Lamb (Rev. 7:10 and 14). Calvary alone is the ground of redemption, whatever the age, and whoever the persons. Chapter 7 is, of course, a great parenthesis. It is to let us see, at the beginning of the tribulation, that God is preparing and preserving His witness for those days. When we arrive at ch. 14 we shall see that that company has indeed been preserved right through, and stands then with the Lamb for whom these saints have suffered in testimony. They are destined for everlasting joy and glory. One day, sinning and suffering, weariness and loneliness, weeping and wandering, will be things of the past. Then they will neither hunger nor thirst, nor want for anything, for the Lamb shall shepherd them; (for such is the word in v.17). Living fountains of waters will be their portion for the millennium and for ever, and God shall wipe away every tear from eyes that must have wept so much during the sorrowful days of their testimony. With white robes, and victor's palms, and songs of joy, their ultimate triumph is sure; and of course, their salvation is honour and glory for the Lamb.

# Chapter 10

## THE SEVEN TRUMPETS

We have seen that the judgments of the Great Tribulation are depicted under a series of Seals, Trumpets, and Vials. Seven seals are broken, seven trumpets are blown, and seven bowls of wrath are poured out. Six seals have been broken in chapter 6, and now, after the great parenthesis of chapter 7, we are brought to the breaking of the seventh seal. Our interpretation of this seventh seal will be determined by our understanding of the relationship between seals, trumpets, and vials. As the final seal is broken, Heaven is silent. What is the significance of this silence? Those who view the seals, trumpets, and vials as consecutive judgments will interpret the silence as the calm before the storm, an ominous silence, and the prelude to more wrath to come. If, however, the seals, trumpets, and vials, are not consecutive, but concurrent, i.e. three different aspects of the same days of great tribulation, then the silence is the silence of judgment accomplished. If the sixth seal, in chapter 6, brought us to the Day of the Lord, the Revelation of the King-Judge, the Great Day of His Wrath, then the seventh seal is the awful intimation that judgment is complete and Heaven rests.

Now we are introduced to the seven trumpeting Angels who are about to sound; but before they do so there is a most interesting interlude at the beginning of chapter 8. Another Angel appears, and stands at the altar. It is a fair principle, that if no other identification is added, then the altar referred to is the brazen altar of sacrifice. Here the Angel receives the burning incense which is to be offered upon the golden altar. There are two altars in v. 3. The priestly character of this ministry

almost certainly identifies the Angel as our Great High
Priest Himself, our Lord Jesus. Only He would have the
ability and capacity and authority to make the prayers of
the saints acceptable, as this Angel does. To the
intercessions of the saints He adds the perfume and
fragrance of His own person and they are accepted. But
note too, that having offered fragrance at the golden
altar, He now takes fire from the brazen altar and pours
it upon the earth. Here is the great principle, that
Calvary not only gives God the right to bless, but gives
Him the right to judge also. His rights having been thus
established, the seven angels now prepare to sound.

The first trumpet brings the most appalling extremes
of judgment; Hail and Fire in a shower of Blood! The
"third part" of things is affected under each trumpet in
this chapter. Is this a reference to the Roman Earth? Is it
the territory of the Beast and apostate Christendom?
Trees and grass are here the subjects of the judgment;
man in his dignity, and man in his weakness, all sharing
in the wrath.

The second trumpet sounds in v.8 and a burning
mountain is cast into the sea. If we interpret the
symbolism correctly, then here is the casting down
among the peoples of some prominent dignitary. The
same figure is used of Babylon in Jeremiah 51:25. Are we
to see here the apostasy of a most influential personage
whose downfall affects the masses (the sea), and also the
very commercial life of men (the ships)?

The third trumpet sounds, and a great star falls from
Heaven. It is the fall of a leading light-bearer and
"spiritual" guide. John Baptist was a burning and a
shining Lamp. So also was this star now fallen. Stars and
lamps are expressive of light-bearing in the darkness. So
the same symbols were used in connection with the
assemblies in chs. 2-3 — they were guides during the
night of their testimony. Now the light to which men

have looked is fallen, in the days of the third trumpet. The whole stream of life is affected (the rivers), and the very sources of things (the fountains). The Star is named "Wormwood." Wormwood is a bitter herb, always used in the Old Testament as a symbol of sorrow (Deut. 29:18; Jer. 9:15; 23:15; Lam. 3:15; Amos 5:7). The bitterness of death is here with the fall of the great One.

In verse 12 the fourth angel sounds, and sun, moon, and stars, are involved in the judgment. These are the consistent symbols of rule and of government, but now, with apostasy of leaders comes the darkness of anarchy, and if the light that is in thee be darkness, how great is that darkness!

In the concluding verse of chapter 8 the "angel" is in most manuscripts an "eagle." He flies through the midst of Heaven anticipating the remaining trumpet judgments, and he cries the three-fold "Woe, Woe, Woe." There is a principle with seals, trumpets, and vials, (and perhaps with the Lampstands too), that they are consistently divided into four and three.

The fifth angel sounds in ch. 9:1, and a star is seen, not "falling," as in the A.V., but "fallen." There may be a reference to the star of ch. 8:10, and it is conceivable that the two fallen dignitaries of the second and third trumpets are, in fact, the Beast and the False Prophet of chapter 13. To this fallen star is given the key of the Abyss. He receives authority to unloose the powers of darkness, just as Peter received keys and authority of a more blessed nature. When he opens the bottomless pit there emits darkness and pollution, and an army of locusts out of the smoke of the pit. It is the rampant demonism of the last days. But the Lord knoweth them that are His, and His sealed servants are immune; but Divine Sovereignty permits the tormenting of men for a defined limited period. The locust-tormentors have the power and fury of the war-horse, the authority of crowned heads, the

intelligence of men, the attractiveness of women, and
the ferocity of lions. They have iron protection, they are
as formidable and irresistible as a charge of cavalry, and
they have the deadly, painful sting of scorpions. Their
intimacy with their King, whose Name, whether the
Hebrew Abaddon, or the Greek Apollyon, means
Destroyer, clearly identifies them as Demons. "Destroyer"
is the opposite and antithesis of "Saviour." Apollyon is
Satan.

As the sixth trumpet sounds, four angels are loosed.
They have been under Divine restraint until the exact
moment arrives. The very hour, and day, and month,
and year, of their awful ministry has been decreed; now
it has arrived. Whether these be elect angels, or evil, is of
little account. Their release, at the Euphrates, Israel's
territorial boundary, is the release too, of an army of two
hundred million horsemen. If we parallel this sixth
trumpet with the sixth vial in chapter 16, then these
armies are the armies of the Kings of the East. Perhaps
the number is not to be taken literally, but symbolic of
immensity and vastness, but it is interesting and
striking, that as long ago as 1965, China alone boasted
that she could field an army of two hundred million
fighting men and women, exactly the number of
Revelation 9:16. The picture is terrible in the extreme.
Fire! Smoke! Brimstone! Horses! Lions! Serpents! Plagues!
Demons! Idolatry! Murder! Sorcery! Fornication! Theft!
As W. Scott remarks — "An astounding picture of
human depravity."

Notice that the heart of man is never changed by
judgment. There may be remorse, and even despair, but
never repentance. Only the sweet influence of gospel
grace can beneficially affect the human heart. Here, as in
the fearful scenes of chapter 16, and consistent with the
principles of Romans 1, it is insisted that "men repented
not."

Before the seventh angel sounds in ch.11:15, there is another parenthesis, and when the seventh trumpet is blown we are brought to the moment of the revelation of the King. The interlude of chapter 10 will teach us that behind all the confusion on earth, and in spite of the apparent triumph of Satanism and the forces of Spiritism, nevertheless, the purposes of God are being wrought out and Heaven is in control.

# Chapter 11

## THE CLOUD-ROBED ANGEL

At the close of Chapter 9 we arrived at a dark, fearful moment in the days of Tribulation, but it is at this darkest hour that God in grace gives to His saints the preview of glory of chapter 10. The events of ch.10 are not chronological or consecutive. The chapter is an interlude; a parenthesis whose visions are a foretaste of what is shortly to come. It is a light at the end of the tunnel; it is the assurance of the ultimate triumph when the darkness is past. This is ever like God, to give to His suffering people encouragements in the midst of sorrow. Visions of future glory have ever been incentives to the saints. Abraham saw the God of Glory (Acts 7:2). Moses endured, as seeing Him Who is invisible (Heb. 11:27). Stephen saw the Glory, in the dark hour of martyrdom (Acts 7:55). Peter, James, and John saw it, just when the rejection of the Master had been announced (Luke 9:22-31). Paul saw it too (Acts 26:13); as did John on Patmos (Rev. 1:12-18). Here, ch.10 is the great parenthesis, which previews the coming of the Kingdom, and the vindication of the Saviour.

We shall understand this mighty Angel as being the Lord Himself. Others may not have it so, but will see this angel as just another of many angels who appear throughout the Revelation. They will advance this interpretation by emphasizing the word "another," and indicating that it is the Greek word *allos*. But their etymological analysis is not sound, and proves nothing. The identity of the mighty Angel cannot be determined by simple reference to this one word (which is often used interchangeably with *heteros*). The context must decide, and there is a description here which can hardly be applicable to any created being, even though he is a mighty angel. As we look at this description in detail, it is difficult to avoid the conclusion that here is a Divine Person, appearing as a Heavenly Messenger — the King Himself, our Lord Jesus. There should be no objection to seeing Him under the figure of an Angel. In this great Book of Symbols we have already seen Him as a Lamb, as a Lion, and as a Priest. We shall yet see Him as a King, a Judge, a Warrior, a Reaper, and a Bridegroom, and if here our Lord appears as an Angel, that is not inconsistent with His Person, or with the character of the Revelation. He is "The Angel of the Lord" of pre-Bethlehem manifestations.

He is clothed with a cloud. How often is the cloud the symbol of the Divine Presence. It was so at Sinai (Exodus 19, but especially Ex. 24:15-18). It was so in the Tabernacle (Ex. 40:34), and in the Temple (1 Kings 8:10-11). On the mount of Transfiguration the disciples feared as they entered the cloud, the bright cloud which overshadowed them (Matt. 17:5; Luke 9:34). In Acts 1, at our Lord's ascension, literally translated, "a cloud took Him in." This Heavenly One then, is robed with the insignia of Deity.

The rainbow is upon His head. Notice, it is not "a" rainbow, but "the" rainbow. This is a reference to the rainbow which we have already seen in ch. 4. The rainbow is the promise of mercy in the midst of judgment. It is the emblem of the covenant-keeping character of God; the faithfulness of the God Who promised (Gen. 9:13-17). At this dark hour of sorrow, the saints may rest in His faithfulness, and be assured by the rainbow which shines through the storm.

His face is as the sun. This description is very reminiscent of chapter 1, where, too, the face of the Lord is as the sun shining in its strength. This is the face which shone in glory on the mount of Transfiguration, but how touching to remember that this is the same face upon which He fell in Gethsemane (Matt. 26:39), and which men struck (Luke 22:64), and upon which they spat (Matt. 26:67). Now, vindication! They shall one day look on Him Whom they pierced, and see the face, once disfigured and marred, now resplendent with glory like the sun itself.

His feet are as columns of fire. The symbolism is clear. Here is strength, immutability, power and might, expressed in holiness, and active in judgment. Our God is a consuming fire. He has the moral and personal right to move in judgment, and He does so with feet which are like burnished brass (ch.1:15) and like pillars of fire.

The Angel has in His hand a little book, open. Is there some connection between this and the great book, sealed, of ch.6? Perhaps there is. There, in ch.6, we were viewing the beginnings of the last prophetic week. Here, in ch.10, we are previewing the end. At the beginning, the book was "great," with judgments to be administered, and much of it sealed. Now, at the end, so much has been accomplished, the week is running out, and the book is "little" and "open," as the mystery of God is fulfilled.

The stance of the Angel is significant and interesting. He puts a foot on the earth, and a foot on the sea, and He lifts His hand to heaven. Is He not claiming back what the first man lost? Millennia earlier, God had given Adam a three-fold dominion. Birds of the air, beasts of the earth, and fish of the sea, were his, and authority was vested in him. This dominion is the subject of beautiful poetry in Psalm 8, cited in Hebrews 2. It was God's purpose that all things should be in subjection to man. But we know the sad story of disobedience and a fall, and now, we see not yet, all things put under man. However, we have already seen a Man on earth, another Man, a blessed Man, crowned with glory and honour. We have

seen, in the Gospels, a Man to Whom wild beasts were
subject (Mark 1:13), and Whom the fish obeyed (Matt.
17:27); a Man at Whose word disease, and demons, and
death, fled. A glorious Man this, before Whom nature
itself, winds and waves, bowed in subjection (Mark 4:37-
41). We see Jesus, crowned with glory and honour. The
world, which failed to recognize Him, will yet acknowledge
Him. He puts a foot on the troubled earth, a foot on the
restless sea, and with His hand lifted into the heavens,
He assumes the authority which Adam forfeited. By the
eternal Creator (Himself!) of that heaven, earth, and sea,
He avows that there shall be no more delay. God, in
mystery, has for so long been tolerant of men and evil;
now, that mystery is finished, and the trumpet of the
seventh angel will declare it so.

John is now exhorted to take, and eat, the little book.
He is told that it will be sweet in his mouth, but that,
when digested, it will be bitter; and it was so. The picture
is clear and explicit. How sweet and precious it is to be
allowed to share God's secrets. How blessed a privilege
that we should be taken into His confidence and be
permitted to know what He purposes and plans for the
world. Who are we; who was Abraham, or Moses, or
Paul, or John, that God should make known His mind
and reveal His heart, and indicate beforehand what He
proposed to do? How privileged are those, to whom His
thoughts have been made known. But — when we digest
those things that we have heard from Him, how solemn.
When we really understand what God intends to do, how
bitter it is. What feelings rend our hearts and spirits,
what sorrow, and even tears, as we anticipate the
judgments that will fall, and the terrors that will come.
As earth rolls on its way, merrily, carelessly, heedlessly,
what manner of persons ought we to be, who know what
is in prospect, and who understand the wrath which is to
come. May we live accordingly, as those who know God's

secrets. May we find the balance between the sweet joy of being in His confidence, and the deep sorrow of understanding what is to befall earth and men, remembering that amongst those men are many of our friends and neighbours, and many children of God's beloved people.

Forth in His Name we go,
A royal priesthood now,
His excellence to show,
To whom as Lord we bow:
From darkness called to wondrous light,
The sons of day amidst the night.

Praying for grace to live
As fits a royal race,
We seek to men to give
The light of truth and grace:
His Name to bear, His will obey,
His steps to follow day by day.

# Chapter 12

## THE TWO WITNESSES

We have now arrived at a chapter where it would be neither prudent nor honest to be dogmatic in interpretation. This section is regarded by many expositors as one of the most difficult in the Revelation. Two witnesses; who are they? Are they literally two men? Can they be identified? What do they minister? When do they minister? Do they actually die? Do their bodies really lie on a Jerusalem street for three and a half days? What is this raising to life again? And this ascension? These are the questions which beg for answers in chapter 11.

But first, there is the measuring of the temple, and the altar, and the worshippers. We have before seen, that, after the rapture, there will again be a temple in Jerusalem, with some measure of divine recognition (2 Thess. 2:4). Here, Jehovah assesses just what is His, in a day of apostasy. The Lord, Who, in the days of His flesh, had purged another temple with a scourge in His hand, now directs the measuring of this temple to determine what is His own. The court of the Gentiles is omitted; it is cast out; given up to the nations who trample the Holy City. Jerusalem is often called the Holy City (Nehemiah 11:1,18; Isaiah 52:1; Matt. 4:5; Matt. 27:52, 53). Israel is only once in Scripture called the Holy Land.

Our attention is now turned to the witnesses. It is interesting that John does not actually see the witnesses in vision. The description which we have of them is not John's but that of the Angel of ch.10, whom we have taken to be the Lord Himself. We shall now look at the relevant questions.

*(i)  Are they literally two men?*

Perhaps the majority viewpoint is that they are. It is pointed out that they are referred to as "two prophets." Much of the narrative may indeed suggest that they are two individuals. But in a book of signs and symbols, as Revelation is, this literal interpretation may not be correct. Is the Woman of ch.12 an individual? or the Woman of ch.17? Is not the Beast of ch.13 a system, and not an individual only? Is the Bride of ch.19 an individual? It may well be that we should not be thinking here of two individuals at all, but of testimony for God in a collective way, in that day.


*(ii)  Who are they?*

Those who interpret the witnesses as actual individuals, and who try to identify them, have suggested the names of Enoch, of Moses, and of Elijah. Enoch and Elijah are favoured by some, because they never died, and because, they say, it is appointed unto men once to die, and that, here, now, they return as witnesses to be martyred and to die, according to the appointment. This argument is not valid. There are many of us who expect that we may never die. "We shall not all sleep." There is then, of course, the similarity between the miraculous powers of the witnesses and those of Moses and Elijah, who also turned the waters to blood, and brought plagues upon men, and caused the rains to cease. Some expositors however, will not be so bold as to attempt identification, but will still see the witnesses as two preaching prophets. Is this necessary? Two witnesses were ever the evidence and requirement of valid testimony (Deut. 17:6; 19:15; Matt. 18:16). Why should we not have here a symbolic representation of adequate divine testimony after the rapture, from a believing remnant of Israel and from saved Gentiles as in ch.7, — a two-fold cord.

*(iii)  What do they minister?*

They are Olive Trees and Lampstands. These are consistent types of testimony and light-bearing. If the Angel of ch.10 is the Lord Jesus, then it is the Lord Jesus who says they are "My witnesses" (v.3). Whoever they are, they must bear testimony to Him. After the rapture, as before the rapture, there is but one Saviour, and one way of salvation by the blood of the Lamb (ch.7). This only they must declare, though despised by men, as their garments of sackcloth indicate.

*(iv)  When do they minister?*

For three and a half years (reminiscent of the Lord Himself) they have liberty to minister. Though despised, and essentially opposed, they enjoy divine protection. Their enemies are restrained, and the prophets administer their heavenly mandate. It is the *first* half of the Seventieth Week. During this period active testimony is possible, and perhaps even protected, by the Beast's covenant with Israel. It is difficult to imagine, as some teach, that such unhindered testimony could obtain during the latter part of the week. Nevertheless, many will see it so, and debate will continue as to the timing of the witnesses' testimony.

*(v)  Do they actually die?*

It is only fair to say that the majority of interpreters will see the witnesses as two literal men who really die. If we take the witnesses to be symbolic of God's testimony in that day, then we may view their savage killing in a two-fold way. First, that there will be literal and actual martyrdoms is clearly taught. God's people will dearly pay for their faith, and blood will freely flow. Many, both Jewish and Gentile, will seal their testimonies with their blood (ch.6:9). But secondly, this may be seen as symbolical of world wide rejection of God's truth in

universal apostasy. In the midst of the week the Beast
assumes Deity (2 Thess. 2:4), demands Divine honours
(Rev. 13:12, 15), and destroys religious Babylon (Rev.
17:16-17). The Beast who initiates the destruction of the
corrupt Babylon will kill too, any liberty that has existed
for true public testimony for God.

*(vi) Do their bodies really lie on a Jerusalem street for three and a
half days?*

In Jerusalem, the centre, the carcase lies fallen. Note
that the expression, "dead bodies" (v.8), is a singular
word "carcase." This adds weight to the thought that it is
testimony in general that is being portrayed and not two
individual prophets. The suppression of their testimony
is accompanied by fiendish glee in the world. There is
international delight that the preaching which tormented
the nations has now been silenced. Earth-dwellers
rejoice. There is an unholy exchanging of gifts and a
making merry among men. Many will see the three and a
half days literally, but may they not rather refer to the
short-lived triumph of the enemies of the Truth during
the second half of the Week. May this not well be a
symbolic way of saying that the three and a half years of
the triumph of the Beast are but as transient as three and
a half days, a fleeting glory indeed?

*(vii) What then, is their Resurrection and Ascension?*

God will vindicate His rejected witnesses. That there
will be a resurrection of martyrs, is true, of course; but
the point here emphasised is that Heaven will publicly
acknowledge the prophets whom earth disowned and
refused. How significant is that word — "and their
enemies beheld them!" And in the same hour of their
vindication their enemies are vanquished, and the God of
the witnesses is glorified.

Here is the end of the second Woe.

The third Woe is the sounding of the seventh and last

Trumpet. But to equate this trumpet, the last in this series, with the "last trump" of 1 Cor. 15:52 is naive indeed. Those who argue so, to place the rapture of the Church at this point in time, and not before the Tribulation, often ask in a sort of irony, "Does last mean last?" Yes, of course; but "last" in one set of circumstances, is not "last" in another. Ask any old soldier, as he talks of campaigns of the past, how many times he has heard "The last post!" Does "last" mean "last"? Then how can a "last" post be heard on many occasions? The answer is simple and obvious, of course; we are talking of different circumstancers and so a last call may be repeated again and again at different times. The last trump of 1 Cor. 15 is the last call to saints in a day of Church testimony. There have been many calls. Calls to service; calls to worship; calls to communion; we wait for the last call —the last trump, to call us up and away to Himself. The seventh trumpet of Rev. 11 is something quite different.

This Trumpet heralds the coming of the King. At last, Divine Rights are being asserted. The King will claim His Kingdom, and reign. In v.18 there is a play upon words which is not apparent in our Authorised Version of the Revelation. "The nations were angry, and thy wrath is come." The words "angry" and "wrath" are the same. The nations are angry, and God is angry. It is a fearful scene. The heavenly Temple is opened; the inner shrine with the Ark of the Covenant — a symbolic reminder that God is true to His covenant promises, and that now, the Kingdom has come. It is the spirit of Psalm 2. God will now reward and avenge His servants, and destroy their enemies, and His Christ will reign "for ever and ever." There may indeed be a thousand years of a particularly earthly reign, but the Kingdom itself never ends. The millennium may terminate, but the Kingdom is the everlasting Kingdom of our Lord and Saviour Jesus Christ (2 Peter 1:11).

# Chapter 13

## THE WOMAN AND THE DRAGON

There are four interesting women in the Book of the Revelation; two of them are good, and two are evil. *Jezebel,* in ch. 2, is, as we have seen, the prophetess of spiritual and moral error. *Babylon,* in ch. 17, we shall see to be the very epitome of corruption and apostasy. In *the Bride* of ch. 19 we shall see the King's companion in glory. Here, in ch. 12, *the woman is Israel.* John calls her appearance "a great sign." He uses this word some seven times in the Revelation, this being the first. The other references are 12:3; 13:13; 13:14; 15:1; 16:4; and 19:20. In our Authorized Version the word is variously translated signs, miracles or wonders, and the thought appears to be that here is something remarkable and extraordinary, a phenomenon in which some important truth is being signified (SIGN-ified).

The woman is clothed with the sun, with the moon at her feet and a crown of twelve stars on her head. We have before seen, that sun, moon, and stars, are consistent symbols of government, and of course there may well be an allusion to Genesis 37, where Jacob and Rachel and the Patriarchs are so seen in association with Joseph. One day the Nation will share the glory of the rule of the Heavenly Joseph, in glad acknowledgement of His Sovereignty. However, it is important to note that this sign is "in heaven;" this view of Israel is heaven's view. It is Israel, not as she is now, nor as she has been, but as God intends her yet to be. But, as is so often the case, that glory is arrived at by an avenue of suffering.

The woman travails. She awaits, in pain, the imminent arrival of her Child. For centuries, in suffering, Israel

75

waited for Messiah. But what is the meaning of this strange verse, Isaiah 66:7? "Before she travailed, she brought forth; before her pain came, she was delivered of a man child." The sad fact is, of course, that Israel's real sorrow is yet to come. Her darkest days and most bitter sufferings are yet to be, and this though Messiah has already come. As we know, her Child came unrecognized. "The world knew Him not." "His own received Him not." He has come, but Israel is unaware of it. The long promised, long awaited One has been, and still the Nation groans, and will groan, until He comes again. Unparalleled tribulation will yet be hers, before her true deliverance comes in the recognition of Jesus as Messiah.

There appears a second sign — a great red Dragon. There is no difficulty with this symbolism; the Dragon is explicitly identified as Satan, the Devil, the Old Serpent. Thirteen times in the Revelation the Devil is called "the Dragon." If numbers have any meaning in Scripture, (and they seem to have), then thirteen is the number of disorder, of anarchy, of defection, and of lawlessness. Indeed, in its first mention in Scripture, the number thirteen is associated with rebellion (Genesis 14:4). Eight times in Revelation we have the name "Satan," and five times he is called "the Devil;" another thirteen then, in relation to the evil one. As Satan, he is the Adversary, or Opposer. As the Devil, Diabolos, he is the Slanderer, or Accuser. The Old Serpent is the cunning, crafty One, whose wiles we know. It is a title reminiscent of Eden and Eve. In the Dragon, however, we see his monstrous cruelty, and perhaps this is nowhere more evident than in that which is called "the slaughter of the innocents." The Dragon stood by when Messiah made His Advent. In the Roman Empire of that day he waited in the person of Herod the Great. His intent was, that by the instrumentality of that wicked King, he would devour, in infancy, the true King of the Jews. Herod was an Edomite, a half-caste puppet King who had received his authority from the Caesar. The Dragon would use him to destroy the infant Christ. But earth's powerful potentates were really helpless, and Heaven's apparently helpless King in a manger was all-powerful. The innocents were slaughtered, and Rachel, Jewish Mother-hood, wept for her children, but Messiah was preserved. In keeping with the context of the passage, Egypt, Nazareth, Galilee, Judea, Golgotha, Cross and Tomb, are all here omitted. The Man Child is "brought forth," and "caught up." Now, in the spirit of Psalm 110 and Psalm 2, God's decreed and destined Ruler waits in the Heavens until the day of His manifestation in power and glory.

Our thoughts are now projected beyond this present mystery period, and we are again concerned with the woman, Israel. The Dragon is wroth, and the woman will suffer at his hand. But she is preserved by a God who numbers the very days of her suffering. It is not here "three and a half years," as in other places; not even "forty two months;" but "a thousand, two hundred and sixty days." The God who wipes away every tear, numbers every day of His people's sorrow.

There is war in Heaven. The opposing forces are commanded by Michael and by the Dragon. Michael, the Archangel, in the five Biblical references to him, is ever associated militantly with Israel. With his angels he now prevails over the Dragon who is cast out. Chronologically, it is the midst of the seventieth week (Daniel 9). It is interesting too, that by a count of verses we have now arrived at exactly the middle of the Book of the Revelation. How thrilling it is, that right in the heart of the story of God's dealings with Israel and the Nations, Satan is defeated and the triumph and glory of Christ is proclaimed, verses 7-10.

But if Heaven rejoices, it is not so on earth. "Woe to the

inhabiters of earth and sea." He who once was "Lucifer," the Day Star, is now cast out of the heavens, to earth. He has drawn with him a third part of the heavenly populace, and now, defeated in the heavens, and knowing that his time on earth is short, he directs his hatred towards the woman in a most fearful way. There will be, in these days of vengeance, a Satanic onslaught against the Jew. We remember, however, that a remnant of the Nation will have acknowledged Jesus as Messiah, and will be preaching the Cross, (v.11). For these there is a double persecution, who suffer because they are Jews, but who also are the special objects of Satan's wrath because they are Christ's (v.17). But the Nation is preserved. The Serpent pours out a torrent of persecution, but in the wilderness of the world the annihilation of the Jew is neither permitted nor possible. In a strange, paradoxical way, world opinion has ever been against Israel, and yet the same world calls out in indignation at the atrocities which have been inflicted upon her. It will be so during the coming travail. Earth will somehow protect the Jew from the venom of the Serpent, and by the ministry of the sealed servants who keep the testimony of Jesus the Messiah, there will eventually be a remnant Nation to greet that Messiah when He appears in glory.

So, in this chapter 12 we have introduced to us several of the chief personalities of the last days. In the next chapter there emerge the two most dominant men of those days — the Beast and the False Prophet.

# Chapter 14

## THE TWO BEASTS

At a meeting of N.A.T.O. in Paris in October 1957, Paul Henri Spaak, the then Secretary General, declared, "We do not want another Committee; we have too many already. What we want is a man of sufficient stature to hold the allegiance of all people, and to lift us out of the economic morass into which we are sinking. Send us such a man, and be he god or devil we will receive him." Popular newspapers reported with banner headlines — "GIVE US A MAN."

What we are about to contemplate in chapter 13 of the Revelation, is, in fact, God's answer to that request. It is a divine account, written almost twenty centuries ago, of the advent of the man for which the nations have clamoured. It is the chapter of the two dominant personalities of the last days; one a political supremo; the other his religious henchman.

John stood on the sand of the seashore. Some think that this should read "He" stood upon the sand, i.e. the Dragon. It is not of great importance and does not appear to affect subsequent interpretation. The predominant sight is that of a Beast emerging from the sea. It will soon become apparent that the Beast is both a system and an individual; both an empire and a man. He is the man who will accept from the Devil what the Lord Jesus refused —power, authority, a Throne, and a Kingdom. "All these will I give thee" (Matthew 4:8-9).

The sea is a consistent symbol of the restless masses of the Nations, and from this restlessness the Beast emerges. But this does not preclude the man being a Jew. Well-known contemporary personalities have proved that a man may well rise up out of the sea of nations and yet be a Jew. Since those ancient people have long been absorbed in Gentile society it is not to be wondered at that from time to time some of her sons emerge from it into prominence. So it is here.

The word "Beast" must not be changed or diluted. It is the word for "wild beast" or "brute." It is not as the word of ch.4 and other passages, which is simply "living ones." This Beast has all the stealth, rapidity, and cunning grace of the Grecian leopard; he has the strength and savagery of the Persian bear; and the dignity, power, and majesty, of the lion of Babylon (Dan. 7). These all combine in the seven-headed monster which is undoubtedly a revival of the ancient Roman Empire. The seven heads are seven Kings, or Kingdoms (Rev. 17:10). These have one thing at least in common; they have all, down the centuries, nurtured mystery Babylon. To see them as successive forms of Roman government is too weak. They are Kingdoms, Empires, most of which are now fallen. Who can they be but Egypt, Assyria, Babylon, Persia, Greece, and Rome of the past. A Rome of the future completes the seven. But this we leave until, God willing, we come to ch.17. Sufficient to see here, that in this monster we have the final form of Gentile dominion, and the world wonders that the head which had seemed to be mortally wounded is resuscitated, and Rome is revived again.

The Dragon, of course, is only interested in the Beast's supremacy inasmuch as that is the vehicle and means by which he himself is worshipped. This was his stated condition in Matthew 4 when he offered the kingdoms to our Lord. "Fall down and worship me," he demanded. Here he receives through the Beast, the worship of the world.

The Beast will be a master orator, and the power of oratory is well known. In his pride and arrogance he will sway the masses. For the first half of the week he may indeed ride the white horse in peaceful bloodless triumph, and carry the woman Babylon with him (ch.17). But in the midst of the week he will be personally energised by Satan, and in blatant blasphemy against God and all gods, he will assume deity, and sit (in the form of his image) in the temple, and receive world-wide homage from all kindreds and tongues and nations. If his Empire will have physical or geographical boundaries, his influence and fame will have none. All that dwell on the earth shall worship him, excepting those who belong to the Lamb. His dominion is therefore universal, and he inaugurates fierce persecution of the saints. But God will eventually and inevitably mete out righteous retribution. "He that leads others into captivity will himself go into captivity; he that kills with the sword must himself be killed with the sword;" and in the trial the saints must wait in faith and patience.

The second Beast rises out of the earth. He completes the evil trinity of this chapter, and is the lieutenant of the first Beast. The "earth" may well symbolise an ordered, settled society; the Land of Israel itself? This is in contrast to the international turbulence from which the first Beast emerged.

It is argued by some that this second Beast is Antichrist, because of his obvious religious characteristics, and because, it is asserted, the first Beast is a Gentile. But we have already seen that a man may well rise up out of the sea of nations and yet be a Jew. How many well known names could be mentioned! Also, is not the first Beast interested in religious matters? Worship and worshippers; temples and deities; what could be more religious than this? The second Beast, the false Prophet, is essentially a subordinate, which an Antichrist will surely never be. He ministers, lamb-like, for the glory of his master, and speaks with the authority of the same Dragon who empowers both of them. There is a fiendish imitation of the mystery of the Trinity; an unseen Dragon, a throned Ruler, and a false Prophet alluring men and directing worship to both.

The ministry of the false Prophet is attended by miracles. Supernatural phenomena, great wonders, and fire from heaven accompany his verbal directives. He has power to give breath to an image of the Beast which will sit as an abomination in the Temple, and the penalty for refusal to worship is the capital punishment, death. Buying or selling, whether domestic purchasing or commercial trading, will be almost impossible for those who will not wear his mark. How difficult and dangerous it will be then for those who bear Another Name in that day. Yet even in the dark days of vengeance, there will be those who will eventually come out of it all with white robes, and with the song of the Lamb on their lips.

The mark of the Beast is well known (and yet unknown!). It is "666". It may well be a literal mark. This is not unknown even today. There are many who now wear a visible indelible mark in their foreheads in honour of their god. Of course it may be something more subtle, more sophisticated, more complex than that. We must be sane and balanced in the realm of symbolism, and avoid sensationalism. Does Wm. Kelly speak for most when he says, "I do not pretend to solve any such question as this. I confess my ignorance as to the number"?

However, we may profitably see in the number, by way of illustration (if not interpretation) that the Beast will, in three spheres, reach as high as a man may. It is not "777". That would be a triple perfection. "Six" is man's number. From the sixth day on which he was created, he has laboured six days in his week, and "seven" has always been just out of his grasp. In three realms, the coming Ruler will just fall short of "7". He will dominate Religion, Politics, and Commerce. If one can control a man in these three spheres of his life, what is left of the man? If a nation could be so dominated, or the world, what is left? The Beast whose number is "666" is a cruel, devilish, despot, who will, in a three-fold way rule in the affairs of men, and so ensure his own supremacy.

But it is only for a little while, until He will come, Whose right it is, and under Whose sceptre a millennial earth will enjoy real and true peace.

# Chapter 15

## THE VICTORIOUS LAMB

It has ever been characteristic of God, in His thoughtfulness, that in dark hours of sorrow and trial, He gives to His people a glimpse of coming glory. This principle is often seen in the Psalms, and in the general history of Israel, and it is also one of the reasons for the Mount of Transfiguration. Here, in the Revelation, it is the same, and by means of several parentheses during the course of the visions, we are encouraged to look to the end to the ultimate triumph of Divine things. Chapter 7 was the first parenthesis; then chapter 10; now in chapter 14 we pause again to look away to the end. How comforting will these great parenthetical chapters be to the saints of those days of tribulation! What encouragement for them to look beyond their sorrows and know that eventual glory is assured.

This chapter 14 begins with a sight of God's glory in His people, and ends with the Harvest and Vintage of judgment which is Armageddon — the triumph and vindication of His Son.

The Lamb (not "a" Lamb, as in our Authorised Version) stands on Mount Zion. Note that "Sion" is "Zion," both here and in the mention of the Mount in Hebrews 12. Zion is almost a synonym for Monarchy, for Royalty, Regality, and David's Throne. It is the Lamb's right to stand here, and to be surrounded by those who sing His praise and bear His character. His Name (and His Father's Name, see R.V.) is upon their foreheads, in glorious contrast to those who wear the Beast's mark in the previous chapter. The 144,000 have been preserved through the Tribulation as was promised in ch. 7. There, at the beginning of the Tribulation, we saw them sealed. Here, at the end, we see that God has indeed brought them through the fire and out of it, to share in the Kingdom Glory of Christ. The 144,000 are not the whole Remnant, but that part of the Remnant which has been preserved from martyrdom. They have been sealed as His servants, and have maintained continuity of testimony through those dark days. Now they join the song of the martyrs. It is the song of redemption. They, and their martyred brethren, lived in purity in the midst of impurity. In a society opposed to the Lamb, they were His followers wherever He directed. In a world system characterised by deceit and falsehood, there was no lie in their mouth. Now, the days of testimony and pilgrimage are over, and they stand unblemished with the Lamb in Kingdom glory.

In verse 6, the first of six angels in this chapter is introduced. He brings the everlasting Gospel. We must not fall into the snare of seeing different gospels. There is ever but one gospel in God's dealings with men; but the emphasis differs from one age to another. John Baptist preached with the Coming of the King in mind and at hand. This was his emphasis, and we rightly say that he preached the gospel of the Kingdom. But our gospel is substantially the same as John's. We denounce sin; we preach repentance; we proclaim, "Behold the Lamb of God." Our emphasis today, however, is not on the coming of the King, but on the great fact of God's Grace which reaches out to Gentiles who had been afar off. Accordingly then, we say, that we preach the gospel of the Grace of God. It is in other places, "The Gospel of Peace," or "The Gospel of God," or "The Gospel of our Salvation," according to what is being emphasised at the time. What then is this, "The Everlasting Gospel"?

It has been called by some, "The Everlastingly-applicable Gospel"! Its basis is the Sovereignty of God

and His creatorial rights. The whole duty and chief end
of man in every age is to recognize this divine authority,
and herein lies the creature's happiness. This is the basic
principle in the gospel in any and every age. Further light
and differing emphases there may be, but acknowledgement of God's rights is a basic eternal principle.

A second angel now appears in verse 8 and pronounces
the fall of Babylon. "Babylon the Great is fallen, is
fallen." This repetition is not just rhetoric or poetry. It is
without doubt a reference to the two stages in the
judgment of Babylon, which will be amplified in later
chapters. Since the days of Nimrod in Genesis 10,
Babylon has been a politico-religious system of evil and
mysticism, opposed to God and His people. Here is
anticipated the fall of it. Religiously and socially it is
doomed, but this doom is the subject of another section
of the Revelation, and we leave it meantime, as it is left
here.

A third angel comes into view and with a loud voice
proclaims the doom of the worshippers of the Beast, and
how terrible is that doom. Unmixed, unadulterated, fury
and wrath; fire and brimstone; endless, restless, torment;
and all this with the acquiescence of the holy angels and
the Lamb Himself. They have worshipped the Beast;
they have borne his mark; and now they bear the
predicted judgment. But how blessed are those saints
who patiently endure and live for God. They keep His
commandments and the faith of Jesus in most difficult
times, and will share in His glory.

A voice from heaven now instructs John to write —
"Blessed are the dead which die in the Lord from
henceforth." How often today we use these comforting
words in times of bereavement. They are, of course, to
some extent true for us today. Those who die in the Lord
are always blessed, in any age. But the word, "from
henceforth," obviously gives them a special significance

for saints of another day. These martyrs have lived and testified in days of unparalleled persecution, and for them, death is blessedness indeed, bringing them into eternal rest and to divine approval and recognition of their labours.

The chapter ends, as we have seen, with a vision of Armageddon. It is viewed as a harvest, and as a vintage. These are very suggestive of "bread and wine," which are so often linked together in our Bible. It is interesting that when bread is first mentioned, alone, in Scripture, it is connected with the curse (Genesis 3:19). Similarly, when wine is first mentioned alone, it is also linked with sin and shame (Genesis 9:21). When bread and wine are first mentioned in association with each other it is with blessing (see the story of Melchisedek and Abraham in Genesis 14). Is this, in Revelation 14, the final suggestion of bread and wine? The harvest of the earth, a parallel with the gathering of the wheat into the garner, as preached by John Baptist. Some will see the harvest as a gathering in for blessing, and the vintage as a scene of judgment. In the context, and in keeping with Joel 3:1 we rather see a two-fold judgment on Israel and the Nations, both of which are full, over-ripe, in wickedness.

Here is the last mention of the title "Son of Man." Do we remember the first time we read it in the New Testament? It was in Matthew 8:20. There too, as here, His head is mentioned. In Matthew 8:20 there was nowhere to lay that blessed Head — it is our Lord in the world unrecognized and unwelcomed. But now that Head is adorned with a golden crown. It is the day of His manifestation and vindication. As a cloud took Him in, in Acts 1, so now, a cloud brings Him out.

Both the Harvest and the Vintage are fully ripe; indeed the Harvest is over-ripe. The Lord will thrust in the sickle, and will tread the winepress alone. When, in Isaiah 63, He appears from Edom and Bozrah in

garments stained with blood, this, of course, is the blood
of His enemies, as in Revelation 19:13. The imagery in
Revelation 14 is horrific. The blood of the slaughter
reaches to the horse bridles on a 200 mile front. This is
roughly the whole length of the Land, and if the furlong
here is the Roman *stadia*, as it appears to be, then the
measurement iş 160 miles — the distance from Dan to
Beersheba. From Megiddo, through Olivet, to Edom, our
Lord tramples the winepress, and vanquishes the
enemies of God. He is the Lord of Psalm 24 — Mighty in
Battle.

I have stood at a vantage point in Nazareth, looking
out across the plain of Megiddo, and thought, "How
glorious, that when our Lord Jesus becomes the Victor of
Armageddon, it will be within sight of His home town of
Nazareth." The Conqueror of Megiddo is the Carpenter
of Nazareth!

# Chapter 16

## SEVEN BOWLS OF WRATH

We have now arrived, in chapters 15-16, at a most fearful section of the Revelation. In chapters 14-16 there are six mentions of the wrath of God. We have already read of the wrath of the Dragon, and of the wrath of Babylon, and of the anger of the Nations. Now we are to see the fierceness of the wrath of God. Chapter 15 is preparatory. Seven angels await the Divine command. As we wait, we are allowed another sight of the crystal sea, of which we have read in ch.4. There, in ch.4, the sea was associated with expressions of God's holiness; thunderings, voices, lightnings, and lamps of fire. But here, in ch.15, the saints actually stand and sing on that same Sea of Glass. In such awful circumstances, and in the presence of Divine holiness, they are unafraid, because the Lamb is there. They join in the music of Heaven.

We must not talk loosely, as some do, of "The Song of Moses and the Lamb." This is not correct. There are two songs, "The Song of Moses" and "The Song of the Lamb." To speak as if it were the one song of "Moses and the Lamb" is to be guilty of the error of the Mount of Transfiguration — "Let us make here three Tabernacles." It is an impermissible equating of Moses and Christ. The import appears to be that the Song of Moses in Exodus 15 was the first recorded song in Scripture; and it was a song of Redemption. The Song of the Lamb is the final, eternal Song, and it, too, is Redemption's Song. From first to last God is concerned with the Redemption of His people. It is His eternal purpose, and we shall sing it forever with saints of every age. We shall praise Him for what He is, and for what He has done; for His mighty acts and for His excellent greatness; and we shall worship and extol Him, not only as the God of Israel, but as the King of Nations too (for such is the correct rendering at the end of verse 3).

The Holy Place is now opened, and the seven angels emerge, arrayed in pure linen, girded with gold and carrying the golden bowls full of God's wrath. The Temple is filled with smoke, reminiscent of Exodus 40 and Isaiah 6, and man is excluded until God in His glory has fulfilled His purposes with the nations.

It is of great interest to follow the movements of these seven angels keeping in mind another seven who blew seven trumpets. The parallel between these two series of judgments must not be missed. The first Trumpet agrees with the first Bowl of wrath; the second Trumpet with the second Bowl; the third with the third, and so on until both seventh Trumpet and seventh Bowl bring us to our Lord's return in glory and to Armageddon. If there is any doubt about the Seals, there is no doubt about the Trumpets and Vials — they are concurrent, not consecutive. It is a fresh, clearer look, at the same period.

In ch.16 the Angels are released for their awful ministry of judgment. They have a Divine commission, for the voice which sends them comes "out of the temple." They carry the awesome burden of the wrath of God. The word "wrath" is "fury." God is angry with the nations. In these end times we must distinguish between tribulation and wrath. The saints may have tribulation, but they are not the subjects of God's wrath. This is poured out discriminately upon the Beast worshippers.

The first angel pours out his bowl of fury upon the earth; the second is poured upon the sea, and the third upon the rivers. The fourth bowl is poured upon the sun; the fifth upon the throne of the Beast; the sixth upon the great Euphrates. The final, seventh bowl, is poured into the air, and this brings the series of judgments to a fearful crescendo. We must observe them in more detail.

The first judgment brings a grievous "sore" upon those who wear the Mark of the Beast. This is our word "ulcer." It may well be a literal, foul, ulcerated affliction. They have borne the Beast's Mark; now God will mark them. They have given to the Beast the homage due to God. They must now bear the terrible consequences.

The second bowl of wrath brings death to the sea. In a fearful, obnoxious symbolism, the sea becomes like the coagulated blood of a corpse. Marine life dies. If the judgment is literal, it is terrible. If it is figurative, it is the death of international commerce. The main stream of trading is stayed.

With the third bowl, the rivers are polluted, and the fountains of waters. The very springs of life are threatened. And lest any should think that such judgment is harsh, the angel of the waters insists that God is righteous in so acting. He is, and was, and always has been, the Holy One. His Judgments are ever true and righteous, and those who receive them are always worthy of judgment. In this case, it is exact and impartial retribution. These men have shed the blood of saints and prophets, and accordingly God turns their drinking water to blood. They have killed His servants; He will kill the streams of their life. Another voice joins in the vindication and proclaims, "True and righteous are thy judgments."

The fourth vial affects the sun, and men are scorched with fire. But still they do not repent. Here is an unchanging principle that men's hearts are not changed by judgment. In the pains of these judgments at God's hand, they persist in blaspheming His Name.

As the fifth bowl is poured out, this principle is emphasised again. The throne of the Beast is assailed; his Kingdom is darkened; his subjects are in distress. Yet in their distress and in their pain, and gnawing their very tongues for pain, still they blaspheme God, and stubbornly refuse to repent.

The sixth angel now appears. His judgment ministry is directed against the river Euphrates, which is dried up. This prepares a way to Israel for the Kings of the East —literally, the Kings from the Rising of the Sun. There is a striking coincidence with the sixth trumpet in ch. 9. There, in verses 14-16, the Euphrates is mentioned too, and an army of two hundred million horsemen. It is interesting, that at the present time China can boast that she can field an army of that same number — two hundred million. There is now an upsurge of demonism. Men and their rulers will be subject to demon possession, having rejected God and His truth. The Dragon, the Beast, and the False Prophet promote this demonism, and as the great day approaches, the armies of earth are on the move. Suddenly, as the coming of a thief, it will all be over. Saints there will be, who will watch, and, walking unblemished in a hostile world will be remembered for blessing. The Nations are gathered, by Divine purpose, to Armageddon — Har Megiddo, the Mountain of Slaughter.

Now, the seventh vial is poured into the air. A loud voice from the Temple cries, "It is done!" There are thunderings and lightnings and an earthquake. Why should not this be literally so. Once before, a similar cry had rent the air, when the Holy Sin-Bearer cried, "It is finished." Earth had quaked then too, and the earthly temple had been opened, and men had trembled. Here, Babylon is divided asunder. As she has drunk the blood of saints and martyrs, she must now drink the wine of the fierceness of God's wrath. Mountains and islands are moved. A fiercesome hail falls, every stone a talent weight. The symbolism is frightening. A talent is usually estimated at 3000 shekels, which may have been as much as 114lbs (Newberry). And still, as before, men blaspheme God. Neither the extremes of scorching fire nor pounding hail will melt the heart or break the will of reprobate men, who will live and die in apostasy. They have rejected God and have given allegiance to the Beast, and their doom is certain.

The ministry of the seven angels is now complete, except that one of them will now show us, in some detail the two-fold judgment of the Great Harlot, Babylon. But this is chapters 17-18.

# Chapter 17

## BABYLON

We have already seen that the judgment of Babylon is a two-fold, two-stage judgment. The doom of Babylon religiously is portrayed in chapter 17. Babylon commercially is destroyed in chapter 18. It is well known that the tentacles of religious Babylon penetrate and intertwine almost every department of commercial life.

But first, perhaps, we should identify and define Babylon, and we must not fall into the common error of equating Babylon with Rome. No doubt if we want to see Babylon to advantage today, it is to Rome that we look. Here she is best and most easily seen. However, Babylon is bigger, and greater, and older by far, than the Papacy or the Papal system.

We must, in fact, go back as far as Genesis 10, to Babel, and to Nimrod, a great grandson of Noah. Nimrod's wife (not mentioned in Scripture) has been called "The first High Priestess of Idolatry." Babel was apparently intended to be "Bab-el," which means "The Gate of God," but God blew upon it and it became "Babel," i.e. "Confusion." Here Babylonish mysteries had their origin. Here is the fountain head of every idolatrous and pagan system which has corrupted the world and plagued Israel.

From Babylon the mystery religion spread among the surrounding nations. The wife of Nimrod was "The Queen of Heaven." Her son Tammuz, who, she claimed, was virgin born, was hailed as the promised Redeemer. The cult of Mother and Child was everywhere associated with mystic rites and ceremonies, and with secrets known only to the initiated. Babylon is the birth-place of priestcraft, purgatory, temple prostitution, and countless sacraments and festivals. Within one thousand years Babylonianism was a world religion. It was from this corruption that the divine call separated Abram. Centuries later Jezebel brought it to Israel. The Nation was polluted with it, until, ironically, God took them into Babylon to cleanse them from Babylonianism. Today, Christendom and the Nations are heavily influenced by Jezebel (Rev. 2:20). Papal and clerical titles and dress are Babylonish, as are so many of the associated practices and festivals. The mysticism will reach its zenith after the Rapture, until, at last, it will be destroyed. This destruction we are now seeing in these chapters.

At this point in the Revelation John's location is changed again, and, appropriately, he is taken to the wilderness. Where better, than in wilderness conditions, to see the doom of that which for centuries has counterfeited the Truth. John is shown the Woman, the great Harlot, sitting upon many waters. The many waters are peoples (v.15); the nations universally have been intoxicated with the fleshly appeal of Babylon. She sits upon the Beast. Gentile world powers have always carried her, and nurtured her. She is arrayed gorgeously in the scarlet and purple so rightly associated with the Papacy and the Vatican. She is gilded with worldly treasures. She has gold, silver, gems, pearls. Her Name is emblazoned wantonly upon her forehead, "Mystery, Babylon the Great, the Mother of Harlots and Abominations of the Earth." The designation "Mother," makes her the progenitor and origin of abominations. She is the source of all idolatries. All corrupt worship has been mothered by her who dates back to Genesis 10. As she has made others drunk, she is drunken herself with the blood of saints and martyrs.

Babylon after the Rapture will likely be an amalgamation, or conglomeration, of every "-ISM" under the sun

in one world Church. Indeed, many of these "-ISMS"
already attend as observers at meetings of the World
Council of Churches (W.C.C.).

John is now directed, in his wonder, to the Beast, and
here it is important to notice a slight change of emphasis
regarding the relationship of the Woman and the Beast.
In verse 3 of chapter 17 the Woman *sits upon* the Beast. It
has been taught from this that she is dominating,
controlling, directing, the Beast. Not so. It may seem like
this at first glance, and indeed, even the Woman herself
may think it is so. But in verse 7 the language is different.
The Beast *carries* the Woman. It is not the same thing.
The Beast is not being dominated by the Woman at all,
but is cunningly carrying her for his own ends. Let her
think she is in control. While she is harnessing the
religious instincts of men, and organizing world religion,
the Beast will carry her. But we shall see that once she
has finally created a World Church, and has united
earth-dwellers in a common worship, the Beast has no
further need of her. This universal worship will now be
directed to Him as he sits as God, and ecclesiastical
Babylon can now be disposed of.

We have earlier noticed the seven heads of the Beast.
They are a double symbol, representing mountains, and
kings. There may indeed, be an allusion to Rome, City of
the seven hills, but it is more than this. Here are seven
regal mountains, seven Empires, seven Kingdoms. They
have this in common, that they have all nurtured
Babylonianism. It is too weak to understand these heads
as being seven successive forms of Roman Government
(as some suggest). "Five are *fallen*." Surely a change in a
form of government from Consuls to Decemvirs, to
Military Tribunes, or whatever, could hardly be described
as a "fall." This is the same word as "Babylon is *fallen*, is
*fallen*" (ch.18:2). It is the fall of an Empire; it is too strong a
word for a mere political or governmental change.

What we are looking for here is a series of Empires, Regal Mountains as it were, that have carried Babylon. Five of these in John's day, were already fallen; one existed then; the other two belonged to the then future. What else, who else can they be but Egypt, Assyria, Babylon, Persia, and Greece. These five had come and gone when Revelation was being written. The sixth, Rome, was then dominant, and this is the Head which has been sorely wounded, as it were to death. But the world will wonder, when, under the ten kings of verse 12, this Roman Empire will be resuscitated. The "eighth" referred to in verse 11 is that same Empire in its final form, i.e. under the personal control of the Supreme Dictator, and not under the ten kings as earlier. These will yield their power to him. The "eighth" is the "seventh" in its last form and phase.

After $3^1/_2$ years of subtlety, deceit, and guile, the Beast will assume Deity and claim Divine Honours (2 Thess. 2:4). The Caesars had done this before him. He will become the object of universal worship. Satan enters into him, and energizes him, as he did with another Son of Perdition (John 13:27 and 17:12). The authority of the ten kings is now invested in him and there is total opposition to the Lamb. But the ultimate triumph of the Lamb and His elect is assured, for He is Lord of Lords and King of Kings.

The ten horns now destroy ecclesiastical Babylon. There is no further need of her, and in fearful irony this inveterate enemy of God and His truth is destroyed by those Kings who oppose the King of Kings. Here is Sovereignty indeed, when God puts into their hearts to fulfil His will. They accomplish His Divine will by effecting the desolation of the Harlot. She is burned in her naked shame and consumed, and God's Word and Will are fulfilled.

However, there remains another side of Babylon. This

is that corrupt commercial side of her, which has ever been so closely linked with the ecclesiastical. This too will be judged. But that is another story, which brings us to ch.18, and prepares us for the Advent of the King in His Glory.

# Chapter 18

## BABYLON — THE FINAL FALL

Ecclesiastical Babylon has fallen in chapter 17, destroyed by the ten kings in the midst of the week, when the Beast reached his diabolical supremacy and entered the Temple. We observe now, the course and character of commercial or social Babylon, until this too has fallen, just prior to our Lord's return in glory.

There is a double metaphor; Babylon is viewed as a Woman and as a City, as are the Redeemed in ch.21. The Kings, in their hatred, have rejoiced to see the end of Babylon religiously, but it is to their advantage that commercial Babylon should be kept very much alive. Indeed it would seem that with the religious aspect now removed, Babylon becomes, more than ever, the haunt and habitation of every evil. Notice the three-fold uncleanness of v.2. Babylon has become the home of demons, the hold of unclean spirits, and the very prison house of every foul and hateful thing emanating from the powers of the air. All find a dwelling in Babylon. The evil sway of the Harlot-City is universal and both merchants and monarchs fill their coffers and wax rich with her luxuries. The saints of that day, as the saints of this day, are expected to be separated from everything Babylonish.

Her sins reach unto heaven. Is there an allusion here to Genesis 11 and the Tower of Babel? Like brick upon brick she builds up the accumulation of her sins, and as surely as God judged Babel then, so will He judge this Babel also. And He will judge with Divine retribution. As she has done, so God will exact accordingly, rendering torment and sorrow for the carnal delights in which she has revelled.

How unlike the true Church is this Babylon. "I sit a Queen," she says, "and am no widow." She does not miss the Beloved. His absence means nothing to her. She lives deliciously and carnally, and suddenly the Lord God will render to her mourning and sorrow and famine and death. "She shall be burned with fire." Oh, the irony and exactness of her judgment. Once Babylon burned Jerusalem; now Babylon is burned. All that she did to Zion, God will do to her (Jer. 51:24), and there is universal lament.

The Kings, the merchants, and the shipmasters cry "Alas, Alas," (v.10), "Alas, Alas," (v.16), "Alas, Alas," (v.19). Soon we shall hear the heavens echo, "Hallelujah"! 'Hallelulah"! "Hallelujah"! (ch.19:1-6).

Commercial Babylon trades in no less than twenty-eight items of merchandise in verses 12-13. These are in seven categories. There are precious stones and metals; fabrics and materials; furniture and vessels; perfumes and spices; luxury foods; livestock and transport; and, finally, the bodies and souls of men. Babylon knows no sentiment. Bodies and souls of men are callously regarded as merchantable as sheep and horses or brass and iron. Such is the character and cruelty of that great system even in our own day.

But there now appears, in v. 14, an expression which is soon to be repeated many times — "No more"! Her days of delicacies and luxuries are over. The King is coming. In one hour her greatness is destroyed, abolished in divine judgment. What awful vocabulary tells the story of that final fall. Weeping; wailing; mourning; lamenting; crying; bewailing; fear; torment; desolation; vengeance; violence. All these words appear in the text that tells of Babylon's final doom.

An angel casts a great millstone into the sea. It is a symbol of the casting down of the Great City, and it is "no more." There is "no more" the sound of music and merriment; "no more" the sound of the craftsman's tool; and "no more" the sound of agriculture. All the sounds of living are gone. "No more" light; "no more" joy. Everything is cold, silent, dead, and dark. Arts and crafts, home and industry, commerce and family, are all affected. How different are the "no mores" of chs. 21, 22, where sorrow and tears and pain and death and curse and night shall be "no more."

This is the end of a Babylon which has killed God's prophets and saints down the centuries, and which has deceived the nations by her sorceries. We now arrive at chapter 19.

"Alleluia," is, of course, the Greek form of the more familiar "Hallelujah." "Hallel" is praise, and "Jah" is a form of the Divine Name Jehovah. Hence the word means, "Praise Jehovah," "Praise the Lord." It is interesting that these are the only Hallelujahs in the New Testament, and that we now have four in swift succession. Why? There is undoubtedly a time and a place for "Hallelujah." Some dear saints lean to one extreme and use the word unintelligently and out of place. Others of us are more conservative, and we restrain ourselves when perhaps we ought not. How glad sometimes we are when there is opportunity to release our full hearts in the singing of "Hallelujah, what a Saviour!" Here in Revelation 19, our New Testament is drawing to a close. Four Gospels have been written, and no "Hallelujah." One book of Church History we have had, with no "Hallelujah." Twenty-one inspired letters from several Apostles to Churches and individuals, and still no "Hallelujah;" and now, four Hallelujahs in six verses. Again we ask, "Why?" It is all so simple and so beautiful. The King is coming! He is coming to be vindicated, to receive His rights and His Kingdom. It is the moment of glory for which Heaven has waited. And, unwittingly, earth has been groaning for this moment too. Now it has arrived. It is the time for "Hallelujah."

The Hallelujahs are suitably divided. The first three have to do with the destruction of Babylon. The fourth explicitly announces the advent of the King. Much people, a great voice, and the first Hallelujah, ascribe salvation and glory and honour and power to the Lord Who has judged the great harlot. "Glory and honour and power"! The very things for which Babylon committed harlotry; they are God's, and He has vindicated Himself and avenged His martyred servants.

But not only is Babylon judged — the judgment is "for ever and ever." It is eternal. Babylon thus judged shall not rise again, and in the knowledge of this they again say, "Hallelujah."

The twenty-four elders now join, and the four living ones to whom we were first introduced in chapter 4. Heaven reverberates with praise. As we have already seen, the three-fold Hallelujah from Heaven is the divine answer to the three-fold woe of earth.

Every heavenly voice now blends for the fourth "Hallelujah." It is a mighty crescendo. A great multitude! The voice of many waters! The voice of mighty thunderings! Heaven exults. The King is coming. The Lord God Omnipotent reigneth. With His Bride He will make His advent, with the armies of heaven in attendance. The Marriage has been effected; the Marriage Supper is now to come; but first, Megiddo, Olivet, Edom, and victory.

# Chapter 19

## THE KING

Three "Hallelujahs" have resounded at the destruction of Babylon. The fourth "Hallelujah" is the immediate herald of the coming King, and an announcement that the Marriage of the Lamb is come.

It is important to see the difference between the Marriage and the Marriage Supper. They are two distinct events. Even in our own day and culture they are separate, though related, events. In Eastern, Oriental culture they were most definitely distinguished, and unless we keep this distinction in mind we shall be in difficulties with some parables, and other scriptures, and certainly with this section of Revelation 19.

The Marriage of the Lamb "is come" — i.e. it has been effected, realized; it is a fact; it is "come." At the Judgment Seat of Christ the Bride has made herself ready. She is beautifully dressed in the righteous acts of the days of her betrothal. While she waited for the coming of the Bridegroom whom she had never seen, she had been weaving the fine white linen garments in which she is now attired for Him. In perfect accord with eastern custom He has come for her, and brought her to His Father's house, and here, in the peace and quietness and joy of that house, the Marriage has taken place. The Marriage supper is now to follow, and for this joyous occasion Bridegroom and Bride will appear together now, and, after assembling a grand procession of guests, all will go in to share the joy and celebrate the Heavenly Union.

At the appearing of the Royal Bridegroom Old Testament saints will be raised. They have rested, and waited for this moment (Dan. 12:13). A remnant on earth has waited too (Matt. 25:1). Now the cry, "Behold the Bridegroom cometh" ... "Blessed are they which are called to the Marriage Supper of the Lamb." Note that it is, "The Lamb." The joy of the Marriage and the Marriage Supper has all been made possible by Golgotha.

Twice in Revelation John has to be restrained from Angel-worship, here, and in ch.22:8-9. Angels are but fellow-servants with our brethren and with the prophets. Worship is for God.

Heaven is now opened; the moment of the Advent has come. How interesting it is to compare Revelation 19 with John 19. From John 19 we may take words which are a fitting title for Revelation 19 — "Behold your King." But the King in John 19 is a King in rejection; a King who wears a thorn-crown and a mocking purple robe. He holds a reed as a sceptre, and the knees that bend to Him are bowed in derision. He is the King who has ridden into the City on the back of a donkey, with a few disciples, and His Throne is a wooden cross. How great the vindication now, in Revelation 19. Royal Robes; many Diadems; a White Horse; a Rod of Iron; and the Armies of Heaven in attendance.

His Title is, "Faithful and True." This He has ever been, but it is especially reminiscent of the days of His ministry. In faithfulness and in truth He taught men and represented God. But the Nation to which He came refused Him. The builders, in their blindness, had no place in their plans for this Stone, and they rejected Him. Now, He comes again. The same Faithful and True for whom they had no room is vindicated, and He is now righteous in judging and making war.

As in ch.1, His eyes are as a flame of fire, infallibly discerning, and impartially judging. He wears adorning Diadems, and a Name profound, that man cannot know.

> But the high mysteries of His Name
>   An angel's grasp transcend;
> The Father only (glorious claim!)
>   The Son can comprehend.

However, He has another Name, and is called, "The Word of God." Thoughts are conveyed by words. Words are the vehicles of thought. As it is with us, so with God, He desires a Word to make known His thought, and Jesus was that Word. All that God has to say, He has said in Christ. Apart from Christ, God has no word for men. Men rejected that Word, but He will come again. Still, God will speak only in Christ.

His Vesture is dipped in blood; the blood of His enemies (Isaiah 63:3). He rides in triumph. Here, again, is seen the sharp sword of ch.1 and the rod of iron of ch.2, and He will crush His enemies as grapes are trodden in a winepress. It is the spirit of Psalm 2, and He that sitteth in the Heavens will laugh. The King of Kings has come, and He is Lord of Lords too. Once He died in shame, and they wrote above His head, "The King of the Jews." He was! And King of Israel too (John 1:49); and King of Nations (Rev. 15:3); and King of Glory (Psalm 24:7); and Prince of Peace (Isaiah 9:6); and Prince of Life (Acts 3:15) and now "KING OF KINGS and LORD OF LORDS." Hallelujah!

An angel stands in the sun. The day has dawned. There is an awful invitation to another supper. The flesh-eating birds of the air are called to prepare themselves for the great supper of God. It is the Judgment Supper. Once before, God had provided a supper, a salvation supper for men, but they had refused. "Come," He had said, but they would not come. Now God prepares a different supper, and those who have spurned the divine invitation to the first supper are now to become the prey of the fowls of Heaven. Kings and

Captains; mighty men and all men; horses and their riders; free-men and slaves; great and small; it is reminiscent of ch.6. Indeed, if Seals, Trumpets, and Vials are concurrent, as we have earlier suggested, this is the same as ch.6.

The rulers of earth enter into an unholy alliance. The Beast is here, from the West. The Kings of North and South and East are here too. They are no longer in opposition but in coalition. They, together, will make war against the little Lamb. At Megiddo the stage is set for the most fearful battle in history, but it is not prolonged. The King has come to Olivet and cleft it in two (Zechariah 12:4). He has made a valley of escape for His beleaguered people. Now He comes to Megiddo. Within sight of His home town Jesus of Nazareth will become the Victor of Armageddon.

The Beast is taken, and his henchman, the false Prophet. In the Old Testament, two men, Enoch and Elijah, went up alive into Heaven. Here, two men are cast alive into the Lake of Fire. Their armies are vanquished. The Battle is over. The fowls of the air are gorged with the flesh of those who have thus died in revolt against the Lord and His Anointed.

> Lo, He comes, with clouds descending;
>   Once for guilty sinners slain.
> Thousand, thousand, saints attending,
>   Swell the triumphs of His train.
>     Hallelujah!
> Jesus comes, and comes to reign.

# Chapter 20

## FINAL JUDGMENTS

In Chapter 20 we are largely concerned with judgment. Although there are no less than six allusions to the thousand years which we call the Millennium, these are indeed but allusions, and not an exposition of the glories of that Age. Such exposition has already been given to us by the Prophets and Psalmists, and is not the subject of the Revelation.

There are three scenes of judgment; (perhaps four). Firstly, there is a preliminary, interim, judgment of the Devil. Secondly, there is a judging by fire of the final revolt against the King, at the end of the thousand years. Thirdly, we have the eternal judgment and doom of Satan. Fourthly, the judgment of the wicked Dead, at the Great White Throne.

We have seen that the Beast and the False Prophet have already been cast into the Lake of Fire, but not for another thousand years will the Devil join them there. God has yet purposes to be fulfilled. Satan will be bound with a chain, and consigned to the bottomless pit, the Abyss. Here we see the futility and fallacy of a literal interpretation of this Book of Symbolism. A Spirit-Being bound with a literal chain? It cannot be. How foolish too, to search for the geographical location of the bottomless pit! There can surely be no doubt that the symbolism simply teaches that the Devil will be confined in a state of utter helplessness, until the purposes of God require his release.

Likewise is seen here too, the absurdity of an A-millennialism which teaches that Satan is bound in this present age of grace. This binding of the Devil takes

place when the King comes. Until then this arch-deceiver
continues to delude and devour, and we are reminded of
his power in the four designations which are here given
to him. These are repeated in exactly the same order as
we had them in ch.12, as if to suggest that the judgment
here meted out to him is consequent upon the victory
over him in that earlier chapter. There is an undoubted
link.

He is the Dragon, cruel and monstrous. He is the
Ancient Serpent, ever cunning and subtle, as in Eden. He
is Diabolos, the Devil, slanderer and accuser of God and
His people. He is Satan, the avowed and inveterate
enemy and Adversary. How sad to remember that he
was once the anointed Cherub, full of wisdom and
beauty, but lifted up in pride and now destined for
destruction (Ezekiel 28:12-19). Lucifer, the "Brilliant
Star," is to be brought down to Sheol (Isaiah 14:12-16).
But meantime, he will be held in the Abyss, and the
world of which He has been the Prince for so long, will
pass under the rule and reign of Messiah.

Verse 4 is not consecutive with verse 3. John is now
given a vision of three classes of saints who will live and
reign with Christ. There are those whom he sees already
enthroned. To this we look forward, who share His
rejection now. Next, John sees the souls of those who
have been beheaded for faithfulness to Christ during the
terrible events of the preceding chapters. He sees them
raised to reign. Thirdly, he sees those who had defied the
Beast, who lived true to the Word of God, and had
refused the Beast's mark and image. These all live and
reign, and thus concludes the several stages of the first
resurrection. Of this resurrection Christ has been the
Firstfruits. Then follows the resurrection of those
believers who form the Church, His Body. Then the Old
Testament saints who are raised at the coming of the
King. Finally, the saints and martyrs of the seventieth

week and the days of the Great Tribulation. The
unbelieving dead will not be raised until after the
thousand years. This waits until verse 12.

It is hardly honest, or consistent, to introduce here
two kinds of "life," or two kinds of resurrection, one
spiritual and one physical. This A-millennialists do, to
support the idea of a general resurrection of all the dead
at one time. How clearly is it stated that there are two
resurrections, of the just, and of the unjust, with a
thousand years between. The first is a resurrection "out
from among" the dead. The other is a resurrection of the
unbelieving dead, to stand in judgment. It is a blessed
thing to have a part in the first, for them the second
death has no terrors. But for those who miss the first
resurrection there is indeed a second death, the Lake of
Fire.

Our thoughts are now projected to the end of the
thousand years of Messianic rule. Satan will be loosed.
(An A-millennial problem! If Satan is bound *now,* as they
teach, what is his loosing? Many A-millennialists confess
to an embarassment here). But why should Satan be
loosed at this stage? One reason must be to demonstrate
the unalterable corruption of the human heart, apart
from grace. We have seen that the unprecedented
judgments of earlier chapters did not change human
nature or produce repentance. Neither will the bliss and
glory and prosperity of the reign of Messiah. When the
Devil is loosed, there are immediately found multitudes
who will rally to his call from the four corners of the
earth. These are the posterity of the righteous who
initially entered the Kingdom (Matthew 25:34). Experience of glory has not changed them. Only a work of
grace can help us.

They will gather to the call of Satan in hosts,
numberless as the sand of the sea. It is a final
insurrection against the Lord and His Anointed. Gog and

Magog of an earlier tribulation day (Ezekiel chapters 38 and 39) were but the prototype of this last revolt. They surround the beloved City, the Capital. But in a moment of time it is all over. Fire from heaven devours them. The Devil is taken, and cast into the Lake of Fire, joining the Beast and the False Prophet, in torment that knows no abatement. "Unto the Ages of the Ages" the judgment continues. It is the strongest way in Greek to express Eternity. Ages of Ages, ever advancing, never ending; as eternal as the God whom they have opposed.

Now is the final assize; the Judgment of the Wicked Dead. The Throne is "Great," and for how many reasons! The Greatness of the Judge; the vastness of the assembled multitude; the enormity of the issues to be assessed. It is a "White" Throne. All is righteousness and purity and holiness. The Dead are assembled impartially, small and great. There is no respect of persons. The judgment is inescapable too. Earth and Sea and Hades give up their imprisoned dead. All must appear to have their judgment reckoned. The Books are opened. All is accurate, and infallible, and beyond dispute. The records are divine. Another Book is opened. It is the Book of Life. It is undoubtedly the Lamb's Book of Life, though not explicitly here so called. Only those who live by the death of the Lamb can escape sentence at this Judgment. The Book of Life is opened here, not that it might be searched for names, but as a demonstration that the reason for a man's appearance here is, that there has been no saving link with the slain Lamb, the Man of Calvary. It is the register of those who rest for salvation on the value of His Blood alone.

The varying degrees of judgment having been divinely assessed (Matthew 11:22 and 24) with heavenly accuracy, and according to what a man has been and done, all are cast into the Lake of Fire. There is no escape. There is no outlet. There is no end. No alleviation. No second chance. No hope. How eternally grateful should we be for the substitute Lamb Who bore the judgment for us. How thankful for that sovereign grace that drew us to Him for refuge. How reverently and sincerely we sing —

"Oh awful day, who would not be,
  Sheltered O Lamb of God in Thee;
Safe at Thy side when wild and loud,
  The shrieks of that unnumbered crowd
Shall rend the heavens and fill the skies,
  Till judgment's doom shall close their cries."

# Chapter 21

## THE HOLY CITY

It would be dishonest not to admit that there are many difficulties mingled with the beauties of the concluding chapters of the Revelation. It would be a mistake, however, to miss the beauties because of an undue occupation with the problems. We shall try to find a balance, facing the difficulties as we contemplate the glory.

That the first eight verses of ch.21 bring us to the eternal state, is very clear. Of that there can be no doubt. The final judgment is over. The old heavens and earth have passed away, and with them the great troubled sea of restless nations. Everything is new, and God is content to dwell with men. It is not now, a "people of God" among men, but *all* men are now His People, and God dwells with them, and is their God. The Holy City is here, forever in the freshness of Bridal beauty. There is an ever-flowing fountain of the water of life, and tears and death and grief and distress are no more. The Throne-Sitter is "Alpha and Omega." The purposes of the beginning are now brought to fruition and fulfilment in a glory which shall never be disturbed again.

As for cowardly unbelieving, the abominable and murdering, the impure and idolaters, the lying and the sorcerers, they have been purged forever from God's creation to die the death that never dies, in the Lake of Fire.

In ch.17, an angel from the seven which had the vials of wrath, had shown John the Woman and the City which was Babylon. Now, an angel from the same seven will show him the Bride and the City, which is New

Jerusalem. It is here we meet with perhaps the first problem in these lovely chapters. Is there now, in verse 9, a retrospection? a going back, in thought, to the Millennium? Or are these subsequent verses consecutive with, and continuous from, verses 1-8? Or does it really matter? Perhaps there is now, indeed, a reversion in thought, and we are to see the City in relation to the Millennium, but if the glory of the City is eternal anyway (and it is) then is interpretation much affected by the questions that are raised? Let us contemplate the glory.

Notice that the Bride is here the wife of "The Lamb." She has been associated with Him Who suffered and was rejected. But the days of rejection are past now, and in company with the Lamb in His glory the Bride is as radiant as a crystal-like jasper stone.

However, the question must now be asked, "Who, or what, is this City/Bride? Is this a literal city? Is it an actual place? Or is it the Church? The Church only? Or is there indeed a measure of all these things in this magnificent closing vision? We shall take the view here that there is indeed a place where the saints dwell, and that the glory of the place and the people are so intimately associated, that to see the one is to see the other. Here is a city and a citizenship; a dwelling-place and a people; a Bride at home.

But while we see the Bride, there are other saints too, in the heavenly society. Abraham looked for such a City, and with him there were others who sojourned as pilgrims here. So many of these died, not having received the promises. Now, in Rev. 21, resurrected, and in bodies of glory, they can hardly have a dwelling place on earth. Their names are here, at the gates of the City, in close association with the Bride.

The City is foursquare. There is length, breadth, and height. Whether it is cubical or pyramidical, it is not possible to say for sure. The symmetry of a cube is perfect; it cannot be improved upon. However it is viewed it is the same. If this be a cube, the vastness is amazing. Twelve thousand furlongs are fifteen hundred miles approximately. If the length, breadth, and height, are multiplied, the capacity is about three and a half thousand million cubic miles (3,500,000,000). Well do we sing —

> "Millions have reached that blissful shore,
>     Their labours and their trials o'er,
> And yet there's room for millions more,
>     Will you go?"

It has been estimated that apart from cubic capacity, even the flat area, i.e. fifteen hundred miles by fifteen hundred miles, is as large as Britain, France, Spain, Italy, Germany, and the half of Russia. It is "A good land and a large" (Exodus 3:8).

Notice how the Gates are impartially positioned. There are three gates on every side, East, North, South, and West. The gates are of pearl; each gate is a single pearl. This alone proves that the description of the City is symbolical or figurative. The City may be literal and actual, but the description is symbolical. Every pearl is the product of a wounded side, born in suffering. There are gates to this glorious City only because of Calvary.

The wall of the City is of Jasper. Its foundations are "pebble-dashed" with precious stones. The general impression of the street and the City is of gold and crystal. There is beauty beyond compare, and wealth incalculable.

There is no temple. God only needs a temple where there is sin. In a sinful world God presenced Himself in a Sanctuary in the midst of His people. Here, in the City, there is no defilement, therefore there is no need for a sanctuary. God dwells with His people.

Neither is there need for sun, or moon, or candle. Neither created light nor artificial light is any longer necessary. There is glory there; the glory of God and of the Lamb. These are the Light of that celestial place. In the radiance of that Light the saved of the nations shall walk, not only millennially, but eternally, and the earthly glory of kings shall pale in its brightness.

> "God and the Lamb shall there
>     The Light and Temple be;
> And radiant hosts forever share
>     The unveiled mystery."

The twelve gates are ever open, for they are always open by day, and there is no night there. But defilement shall never enter. Abominable things, that have before disturbed God's rest are excluded here, and this has all been assured by the Cross. The Register of the City is the Lamb's Book of Life.

There is, then, no curse, no sea, no pain, no sorrow, no crying, no tears, no night, no sun, no moon, no candle, no temple. It will be glory and beauty, and light and love. It is indeed, a *New* Jerusalem, a *Holy* City, and a *great* City, and for us, it is, Home.

> "O bright and blessed scenes,
>     Where sin can never come;
> Whose sight our longing spirit weans
>     From earth, where yet we roam.
> Glory supreme is there,
>     Glory that shines through all;
> More precious still that love to share
>     As those that love did call."

                                        (J.N.D.)

# Chapter 22

## CONCLUDING VISIONS

We have now come to the chapter of final revelations in a Book which is all Revelation. It is a chapter of great variety. There is glory and gloom, blessing and warning, promise and prayer.

After the Book of Life in chapter 21:27, we are now introduced to the River of Life and the Tree of Life. All is Life here, because the curse that brought Death in all its forms is now no more. The crystal stream has its source and origin in the Throne of God. Where God's rights are fully known and acknowledged there is Life. And it is interesting and touching that in these last visions of the Throne it is "The Throne of God and of the Lamb." The death of the Lamb has vindicated that Throne and ensured Life in the eternal state. God and the Lamb are enthroned. At the Throne we have our last vision of the Lamb.

The Tree of Life is a collective term. We must not try to imagine one solitary tree in the midst on every side. As we may perhaps say, "The apple tree grows well in such and such a country," meaning the apple tree as a "kind," so here, the Tree of Life, in the vision, grows along the street and by the river, on this side and on that side, in abundance, and produces its fruit with profuseness and regularity every month.

The leaves of that tree are for the health of the Nations. It is not "healing," as if implying sickness that needs to be remedied. There is no sickness then. These are health-giving foliage ensuring that the ills of former days do not recur now, nor forever. The curse, with all its sad implications, is gone, and shall not exist any more.

His servants shall serve Him; not in arduous toiling, but in willing, delightful, happy service, which is a joy. If these servants are sons, that does not preclude service, for even that Blessed One was a Servant-Son. In the joy of that service we shall gaze on Him. We shall contemplate, with unclouded vision, the Face of Him Whom we have loved for so long without seeing; and as we look on Him, His likeness will be, for His pleasure, imprinted upon us. "His Name shall be on their foreheads."

In that glorious place the light is unfading and the day unending. But it is a divine light, independent of either Sun or Lamp. It is the Lord God Who shines upon them.

Like the Christ Himself, the words given to John are, "Faithful and True." They are the words of the God of the prophets, Who for so long spake to men and through men, conveying His Mind, but now the consummation has come. Blessed is that man whose life is ordered by the words of prophecy.

For a second time (see 19:10) John falls to do homage to an angel. Again he is reminded that even the angels are but fellow-bondmen. Homage is for God alone.

The time is near now. The unsealed Book is given to men, and men will be judged according to their response, or lack of it, to the revelation of God. The coming of the Lord will settle destinies for the righteous and unrighteous alike. Happy are those, who, when He comes, are found with white robes, for this is the right to the Tree of Life and the Glory, and all outside is uncleanness and sin.

"Alpha and Omega" of v.13, is "Jesus" of v.16. All the purposes of God, the beginning and the ending of them, are in Jesus. He is the Root of David, because He was before David, and He is the Offspring of David, because He came after David and from David's line; and when He came, He came to David's town. Here, however, He is not the Sun of Righteousness but the Morning Star. The

Church waits for Him as such, but as such He will not be known to Israel or to the Nations. As we wait for Him, and look for Him, we watch the horizon and say, "Come!" It is the voice of the Spirit in the Bride. This is not a gospel invitation. We shall have that shortly. This is a cry from a waiting Church to her absent Lord — "Come!" Let every saint who hears join in the call. We long for Him. We yearn for Him. We cry — "Come!" But now we look about, and think of others. Is there yet a soul around with no Saviour? a thirsty one? Let him come, and whosoever he be let him take the water of Life. Gratuitously, freely, it is available still to him who will but come to Christ.

The last warning of our Bible now is sounded. Let no man tamper with the inspired volume. Let no man dare to add, or detract, from what God has written. If a man so dares, God shall add judgment to him, and deny him any part in the Life of that City.

The last promise follows. How many promises we have had in sixty-six books of Holy Scripture. Here is the last one; and how sweet, "Surely I come quickly." May we each, and all, be able to join, unhesitatingly, unreservedly, in the concluding prayer of all scripture, "Even so, come, Lord Jesus." May we be so weaned from earth's things, so willing to leave them at any moment, that we can say resolutely with John, "Amen, come, Lord Jesus."

The grace of our Lord Jesus Christ be with you all.

> "Lord we shall see Thee as Thou art,
>     In all Thy glory there;
> We shall behold Thee face to face,
>     Thy glorious image bear.

With what delight, what wond'ring love,
  Each thrilling heart shall swell,
When we, as sharers of Thy joy,
  Are called with Thee to dwell."